# Prayer

# &

# Fasting

- ☑ **Purpose**
- ☑ **Preparation**
- ☑ **Action**
- ☑ **Result**

*by*

## Dr. Kingsley Fletcher

Dr. Kingsley Fletcher
P.O. Box 52209
Durham, NC 27717-2209

**Destiny Image® Publishers, Inc.**
**P.O. Box 310**
**Shippensburg, PA 17257-0310**

ISBN 1-56043-070-2

For Worldwide Distribution
Printed in the U.S.A.

Seventh Printing:   1997      Eighth Printing:   1997

This book and all other Destiny Image, Revival Press, and Treasure House books are available
at Christian bookstores and distributors worldwide.

For a U.S. bookstore nearest you,
call **1-800-722-6774.**
For more information on foreign distributors,
call **717-532-3040.**
Or reach us on the Internet: **http://www.reapernet.com**

# *Dedication*

I dedicate this book to the Church of the Lord Jesus Christ and to a new and modern generation that has not had the privilege of being taught the principles of biblical prayer and fasting.

In this time of global change, may the wind that is blowing across the world visit this present generation and the generations to come with a return of true prayer and fasting. May the fire of God revisit the Church and the desire of the Church be rekindled to take up this forgotten and neglected principle.

May the leaders of this new generation restore the true purpose of spirituality to our nations, through prayer and fasting, until the whole world knows that Jesus is King and Lord over the earth.

May the dedication of this book salute the relatively unknown spiritual leaders of the third-world whose efforts and dedication in prayer and fasting have stopped the approach of unforeseen evils in their respective nations. These are men and women who may never be covered by the media, may never be interviewed by a journalist, and may never have their messages published.

I dedicate this to all those who have a desire to see the glory of God revealed in the Church and throughout all the nations of the world. May His Kingdom come and His will be done on earth.

# *Acknowledgments*

My sincere thanks to Jacob and Esther Victoria, my parents and mentors, for the input and training they gave me while I was young. I wouldn't have made it without their godly support.

I wish to thank the associate pastors, ministers, staff and body of Miracle Life Christian Center for their love, daily encouragement and maturity in allowing me to fulfill the plan of God for my life.

I want to thank one of my best friends, Dr. Myles Munroe for encouraging me to put this message into a book and make it available to the world.

Most of all, I thank the Lord for His grace that abounds towards us.

# Table of Contents

Introduction

*And when they were come to the multitude, there came to him a certain man, kneeling down to him, and saying, Lord, have mercy on my son: for he is lunatick, and sore vexed: for ofttimes he falleth into the fire, and oft into the water. And I brought him to thy disciples, and they could not cure him.*

*Then Jesus answered and said, O faithless and perverse generation, how long shall I be with you? how long shall I suffer you? bring him hither to me. And Jesus rebuked the devil; and he departed out of him: and the child was cured from that very hour.*

*Then came the disciples to Jesus apart, and said, Why could not we cast him out?*

*And Jesus said unto them, Because of your unbelief: for verily I say unto you, If ye have faith as a grain of mustard seed, ye shall say unto this mountain, Remove hence to yonder place; and it shall remove; and nothing shall be impossible unto you. Howbeit **this kind goeth not out but by PRAYER AND FASTING.***

Matthew 17:14-21 KJV

# Introduction

The question which the disciples asked Jesus that day was very logical: *Why couldn't we do that? Why couldn't we heal that boy? What is Your secret?* Jesus' answer was very clear. And what He taught His disciples that day is for all believers of all ages:

> *This kind goeth not out but by prayer and fasting.*
> Matthew 17:21 KJV

The type of miracle needed by this man and his son — this kind of healing, this kind of deliverance — will not be realized by those who are self-centered and indisciplined. Only those who are willing to learn how to effectively pray and fast and seek the face of God will experience the power of God manifested in this way.

I am convinced that one of the reasons the twentieth century church is so powerless is that it has lost this godly custom of prayer and fasting and has succumbed to the sins of gluttony and selfishness. If we are to see revival in these last days, if we are to put down the kingdoms of Satan and see the power of our God prevail, those who call themselves "believers" must learn to crucify their flesh so that their spirit-man can commune in liberty with our heavenly Father. And the only way that this can be accomplished satisfactorily is through prayer and fasting.

Together, let us examine the reasons that so many people no longer fast. Let us examine the need for prayer and fasting; and let us examine some practical methods for effective prayer and fasting. Let us move, step by step, into the presence of God so that His power can once again be manifested in your life.

As you read the pages of *Prayer and Fasting*, don't be in a hurry. Take time to carefully assimilate every chapter. Let the message of the book settle down into your spirit. It is simple; but it is powerful. Many of your problems can be resolved by a return to the biblical practice of prayer and fasting. Take time to learn this lesson well.

May our God use the pages of this book (which He has so powerfully laid upon my heart to write) to stir YOUR soul to do whatever is necessary to seek the face of the heavenly Father — while He may be found.

*Kingsley A. Fletcher, Ph.D., Th.D.*
*Chapel Hill, North Carolina*

# Part I

# Why I Still Believe
## in
## Prayer and Fasting

# Chapter 1

## *My Personal Experience*
## *with*
## *PRAYER AND FASTING*

*I tell you the truth, anyone who has faith in me will do what I have been doing. He will do even greater things than these, because I am going to the Father. And I will do whatever you ask in my name, so that the Son may bring glory to the Father. You may ask me for anything in my name, and I will do it.*

John 14:12-14

What powerful words! Growing up in Africa, we believed these precious promises of God and experienced them in our daily lives. Now, after many years have passed, I am convinced that God worked so powerfully in our lives because of our dedication to a life of prayer and fasting.

Some of my earliest memories are of my father taking a bottle of water and leaving the house so that he could find a solitary place to seek the face of God in extended prayer and fasting. He didn't go to a hotel. He preferred an unused stretch of beach where he could spend several days in God's presence. When he returned, I could see the anointing of God on his life.

My nephew Leonard had a serious health problem when he was young. He had something like epilepsy. I was there the day Daddy took Leonard aside and laid hands on him. He said, "In the name of Jesus Christ be healed." From that day on, Leonard never suffered another attack, and today he is a preacher of the Gospel.

God also gave me a praying mother. She has prayed for hours every day since I can remember. Prayer is her bread. Since she has lived with us, I have never known her to spend a complete night in sleep. Every night I hear her praying. At three o'clock she is praying. At four o'clock she is praying. At five o'clock she is praying. She is always praying.

The dedication of my parents to a life of prayer and fasting kept me from going the way of the world, saved my life on many occasions, and put me on a straight course toward the ministry.

When I was only six, I was hospitalized with a serious eye injury. It was so severe that I was in a state of unconsciousness for three months and had to be fed intravenously. Three specialists — one from Germany, one from England, and one African — all gave up hope for my recovery. One of them told my mother: "I am very sorry. There is no hope for your son."

When my mother heard that dreaded verdict, she began walking all over the hospital, talking to God and interceding on my behalf. God told her that if she would enter into a period of serious prayer and fasting, He would spare my life. She obeyed God, and I miraculously recovered.

> The dedication of my parents to a life of prayer and fasting kept me from going the way of the world, saved my life on many occasions, and put me on a straight course toward the ministry.

When I was only ten, I made a determination to follow God and to live an exemplary life, as my parents had lived before me.

At the age of fifteen, I was one of seven teenagers who formed what we called: The Power House Evangelistic Ministries. Our goal was to go from village to village, city to city and school to school, leading people to Christ.

Soon after we formed that group, I was led to enter into a three-day period of prayer and fasting for the first time. If God could use my parents, He could use me. I would seek His face until I heard from Heaven and until His touch was upon my life.

During those days, I attended a meeting in the bush about three miles from my home. There I lay on my face before God and waited expectantly to know God's voice and to get clear directions. I desperately needed to know His perfect will for my life. I was afraid to move to the left or to the right without knowing His desire. I told God that I would rather die than live without His blessing on my life.

Some people may think that such words, uttered by a fifteen-year-old, are not very important. Believe me, they are important to God. It is because of that prayer that I am where I am today. God revealed Himself to me during those days. One night in a service I had a glorious experience. As we were praying together in the church, I experienced what is known as a "trance." In old-fashioned Pentecostal terms, I "went out under the power of God." For the next three hours I was caught up in the Spirit. Other people were praying around me, but I was oblivious to what they were doing or saying. That night I had an encounter with the Lord that changed my life and my ministry; I saw the Devil for the first time for who he really is. It was also during this encounter that I received an anointing to pray for the sick. From then on, I had a new sense of urgency and a new sensitivity to the Spirit of God.

When I got up, someone asked me, "What happened? You were talking, but we couldn't understand what you were experiencing." I tried to explain to them, the best way I could, what God had done in those three hours. I had been in the presence of God, and the experience forever changed the course of my life.

So, very early in life I began to notice the powerful effect dedicated prayer and fasting has on the Christian life. I witnessed yokes being destroyed and heavy burdens being undone and the works of the Enemy being brought to nought — all because someone had fasted and prayed and sought the face of God.

My parents were never afraid of Satan or his hoards of demons. They approached him under the anointing of the Holy Spirit. He respected them. When they spoke to him to go, he could only answer, "Yes sir! Yes ma'am!" He could not resist them and had to submit to their authority.

No wonder Satan tries to keep us from fasting! No wonder he offers every conceivable excuse to the flesh! No wonder he lulls God's people to sleep! He hates prayer and fasting.

When Christianity first came to our part of Africa, we didn't have any fancy meeting places no any buildings that would accommodate us. We met in the bush to sing the praises of God. Sometimes we gathered and prayed all night. During the night it might rain — except in the spot where we were gathered. God protected us.

Many of our outdoor crusades were likewise threatened by rain. When it happened, we commanded the rain to wait until the meeting had ended, and it did. We had such simple faith in God, and He honored our faith.

Some years ago, when a group of other Americans went with me to Africa for meetings, they saw a demonstration of this faith in action. Heavy rains came during our stay and threatened to disrupt our outdoor activities. The archbishop in charge, Benson Idahosa of Nigeria, boldly declared on national radio and television that the crusade would not be suspended and that rain would not interfere with what God wanted to do.

During the meeting cripples got up and walked; blind people were able to see for the very first time; and other outstanding miracles were performed in the name of the Lord. It was already raining in other parts of the city, but we were spared so that God could work in the lives of the great crowd of people who had gathered. When we had said the final "amen" of the crusade, it began pouring rain and everyone had to scurry for cover. This is typical of the simple miracles that God does on the African continent in answer to the simple faith of the African believers.

The miracles that we saw in Africa were not the result of a well-developed theology. We had few text books. What God did was a result of our dedication to a life of seeking the face of God and His will for our lives.

When we read His Word, we believed it; and He performed it. John 14:12-14 was one of our favorite passages from the Bible.

> *Verily, verily, I say unto you, He that believeth on me, the works that I do shall he do also; and greater works than these shall he do; because I go unto my Father. And whatsoever ye shall ask in my name, that will I do, that the Father may be glorified in the Son. If ye shall ask any thing in my name, I will do it.*
>
> John 14:12-14 KJV

The 14th chapter of John is very commonly used in funeral services. Most pastors, however, read only the first part. They dwell on the future promises. "We might not understand it all now," they say, "but in the sweet by and by, we shall meet on that glorious shore. Oh, Lord God, prepare us a cabin in glory land."

Jesus did say:
*"Do not let your hearts be troubled. Trust in God; trust also in me. In my Father's house are many rooms; if it were not so, I would have told you. I am going there to prepare a place for you. And if I go and prepare a place for you, I will come back and take you to be with me that you also may be where I am."*
                                        John 14:1-3

And those words are just as valid today as when He spoke them to His disciples. But He also said:

*"I tell you the truth, anyone who has faith in me will do what I have been doing. He will do even greater things than these, because I am going to the Father."*
                                        John 14:12

And those words are also valid. If we believe in Jesus, we should expect to see the same miracles that He had in His ministry. We are to continue His ministry in the earth.

Jesus established the Church based on His miracle-working power. A church that never experiences miracles is not the Church that Jesus established. Religion without the supernatural is dead. God hasn't changed. He still wants to bless His people. He said, *"He will do even greater things than these, because I am going to the Father."* He promised *"greater things,"* not lesser works. We should expect and receive *"greater things."*

He said:

> *And I will do whatever you ask in my name, so that*
> *the Son may bring glory to the Father.*    John 14:13

*"Whatever you ask!"* That is a powerful promise; and I
believe it. Jesus said:

> *You may ask me for anything in my name, and I will*
> *do it.*                                           John 14:14

*"Anything!"* Praise God! *"Anything!"* That is what our
God has promised. He said, *"I will do IT."* What is this
*"IT"*? This *"IT"* refers to *"anything"* we ask our heavenly
Father in prayer.

In some churches, the pastors are afraid to talk about the
supernatural. It upsets some people. They don't like to
hear about deliverance and healing. As a pastor, I cannot
stop preaching these things — no matter whom I offend.
Sick people still need healing. Bound people still need
deliverance. And God is still in the healing and delivering
business. If that offends someone, I am sorry. I can't
change it.

Jesus repeated this promise:

> *In that day you will no longer ask me anything. I tell*
> *you the truth, my Father will give you whatever you*
> *ask in my name. Until now you have not asked for*
> *anything in my name. Ask and you will receive, and*
> *your joy will be complete.*            John 16:23-24

*"Whatever!"* What a powerful word! That is what God has promised to those of us who believe Him. He tells us to ask, *"that your joy will be complete."* He is concerned about our true needs. He doesn't want us to be without the fullness of joy. He commands us, *"Ask"* so that our joy *"may be complete."*

And when we ask, we should expect to receive what we ask for. His promise is: *"You will receive."* What will we receive? *"Whatever"* we ask in His name. This is God's promise. We should never be surprised when God works a miracle for us. We should expect to see the signs and wonders of God in our midst.

Growing up in the simplicity of African life, it seemed to us the most logical thing to believe and receive what God had promised.

Later in life, I witnessed the tragedies of those who had forgotten to pray and fast and seek the face of God:

We once had a very simple woman of prayer in Africa for whom God did outstanding miracles. She had never attended seminary and had no college degree. But she was powerful in God. After she had spent time in a certain place in prayer, sick people who came to that place would be healed. People who came there with serious problems were delivered.

When foreign missionaries came and saw what was happening in the life of this woman, they convinced her to travel with them to Europe and the United States. They made merchandise of her gift, using her to raise money. Soon her special anointing departed. She weeps for those days, but they do not return. She forgot how to wait upon God in prayer and fasting.

Another African that we know came to the United States from Kenya, where he had been mightily used of God. When he came to America, however, it wasn't long before the miracles ceased in his life and ministry. The lure of riches caused him to compromise his anointing. Later he found it difficult to even remember the mighty things that God had done for him. They seemed like a faraway dream.

When he came to visit us, I felt led to ask him if he would join me in fasting three days. He did. At the end of that time, he told me what had happened to him.

When he arrived in America, everyone offered him food. He was told, "This is our custom." When he wanted to fast, his hosts objected, saying that it would be offensive to fast. "This is America," they said. "Enjoy our American hospitality. You can fast some other time." It was the same everywhere he went. Before long, he had given up his habit of regular fasting, and his anointing began to fade.

Looking back now, I realize that we can maintain a simple faith in God and experience His miracles on a regular basis only if we are dedicated to a life of prayer and fasting. This is the reason, despite the fact that so many Christians have abandoned the custom, that **I still believe in prayer and fasting.**

# Chapter 2

## *The Biblical Basis*
## *for*
## *PRAYER AND FASTING*

*Jesus, full of the Holy Spirit, returned from the Jordan and was led by the Spirit in the desert, where for forty days he was tempted by the devil. He ate nothing during those days, and at the end of them he was hungry.* Luke 4:1-2

It is difficult to understand why so many Christians have abandoned the practice of prayer and fasting. Nothing could be more clearly taught in the Bible.

Moses fasted.

*Moses was there with the Lord forty days and forty nights without eating bread or drinking water. And*

*he wrote on the tablets the words of the covenant —*
*the Ten Commandments.*                    Exodus 34:28

Elijah fasted.

*So he got up and ate and drank. Strengthened by that*
*food, he traveled forty days and forty nights until he*
*reached Horeb, the mountain of God.*    1 Kings 19:8

Ezra fasted.

*Then Ezra withdrew from before the house of God and*
*went to the room of Jehohanan son of Eliashib. While*
*he was there, he ate no food and drank no water,*
*because he continued to mourn over the unfaithful-*
*ness of the exiles.*                          Ezra 10:6

Daniel fasted.

*I ate no choice food; no meat or wine touched my lips;*
*and I used no lotions at all until the three weeks were*
*over.*                                      Daniel 10:3

I know that all of these men lived in Old Testament
times; but fasting continued in the New Testament. Anna
fasted.

*And then was a widow until she was eighty-four. She*
*never left the temple but worshiped night and day,*
*fasting and praying.*                        Luke 2:37

Cornelius fasted.

> *And Cornelius said, Four days ago I was fasting until this hour; and at the ninth hour I prayed in my house, and, behold, a man stood before me in bright clothing,*
>
> Acts 10:30 KJV

Early church leaders fasted.

> *While they were worshiping the Lord and fasting, the Holy Spirit said, "Set apart for me Barnabas and Saul for the work to which I have called them."*
>
> Acts 13:2

> *Paul and Barnabas appointed elders for them in each church and, with prayer and fasting, committed them to the Lord, in whom they had put their trust.*
>
> Acts 14:23

Paul fasted.

> *For three days he was blind, and did not eat or drink anything.*                    Acts 9:9

After he was converted on the road to Damascus, God led Paul to fast for three days — without food and without drink. At the end of that time, God revealed to a disciple named Ananias that he should go and minister to "Saul of Tarsus"; and Saul, now Paul, received his healing and the beginnings of a miracle ministry that would take him all over the then-known world doing the works of God. He never forgot the lesson of prayer and fasting and later told the Corinthians, in his second letter, that he had been *"in fastings often"* (2 Corinthians 11:27 KJV).

Since he wrote much of the New Testament, we look to the Apostle Paul for much of our New Testament theology. He personally founded many of the first churches and taught their leaders. He believed very strongly in the effectiveness of prayer and fasting and practiced it himself.

Most important of all to us, Jesus fasted.

> *And Jesus being full of the Holy Ghost returned from Jordan, and was led by the Spirit into the wilderness, Being forty days tempted of the devil. And in those days he did eat nothing: and when they were ended, he afterward hungered.*                    Luke 4:1-2 KJV

Jesus was wise enough to know that without the Father He could do nothing. He sought the Father in prayer and fasting. He waited in the Father's presence until He was endued with power. How can we do less?

Many people believe that it is impossible to fast as Jesus did on this occasion, for forty days. They think that anyone who tries to fast that long will die. But Jesus wasn't the only person in the Bible to fast forty days. Moses and Elijah did it too. Many people have done it in modern times and have not died. I have fasted forty days, and I didn't die. And you won't die either — if God tells you to go on an extended fast.

The secret of all these men and women in the Bible is that they were involved in the business of God's

Kingdom. When you get involved with Kingdom business, you forget to eat sometimes. You have more important things to think about. Your own wants become much less important to you.

All the great reformers of the church carried on this biblical tradition. They were people of prayer and fasting. They learned the secret of seeking God.

---

Jesus was wise enough to know that without the Father He could do nothing. He sought the Father in prayer and fasting.

---

If you want God's blessing for yourself and for your family, you too will make prayer and fasting a regular part of your life. Now, that we have laid the biblical foundation for prayer and fasting, let us discover why most Christians have abandoned the practice and why we should continue this blessed tradition.

# Part II

# Why Most Christians No Longer Practice Prayer and Fasting

## *Introduction to Part II*

The teaching of prayer and fasting seems oddly out of place in our modern-day setting. Because of that, millions of Christians have lost the habit of prayer and fasting and most of our young believers have never learned to fast. This is a tragedy that saddens the heart of God and delights our common Enemy.

God is saddened because He knows that prayer and fasting can make us powerful in the Spirit. Satan is delighted because, without the power of the Spirit of God, we can never stand against him.

Why have a great majority of believers abandoned the practice of prayer and fasting? Let us examine some of the major causes.

# Chapter 3

## *The Lack of Results in the Past*

*"Shout it aloud, do not hold back.*
*Raise your voice like a trumpet.*
*Declare to my people their rebellion and to the house of*
*Jacob their sins.*
*For day after day they seek me out;*
*they seem eager to know my ways,*
*as if they were a nation that does what is right*
*and has not forsaken the commands of its God.*
*They ask me for just decisions*
*and seem eager for God to come near them.*
*'Why have we fasted,' they say,*
*'and you have not seen it?*
*Why have we humbled ourselves,*
*and you have not noticed?'*

*"Yet on the day of your fasting, you do as you please
and exploit all your workers.
Your fasting ends in quarreling and strife,
and in striking each other with wicked fists.
You cannot fast as you do today
and expect your voice to be heard on high.
Is this the kind of fast I have chosen,
only a day for a man to humble himself?
Is it only for bowing one's head like a reed
and for lying on sackcloth and ashes?
Is that what you call a fast, a day acceptable to the
LORD?*

*"Is not this the kind of fasting I have chosen:
to loose the chains of injustice
and untie the cords of the yoke,
to set the oppressed free and break every yoke?
Is it not to share your food with the hungry
and to provide the poor wanderer with shelter —
when you see the naked, to clothe him,
and not to turn away from your own flesh and blood?
Then your light will break forth like the dawn,
and your healing will quickly appear;
then your righteousness will go before you,
and the glory of the LORD will be your rear guard.
Then you will call, and the LORD will answer;
you will cry for help, and he will say: Here am I.*

*"If you do away with the yoke of oppression,
with the pointing finger and malicious talk,
and if you spend yourselves in behalf of the hungry
and satisfy the needs of the oppressed,*

*then your light will rise in the darkness,*
*and your night will become like the noonday.*
*The LORD Will guide you always;*
*he will satisfy your needs in a sun-scorched land*
*and will strengthen your frame.*
*You will be like a well-watered garden,*
*like a spring whose waters never fail.*
*Your people will rebuild the ancient ruins*
*and will raise up the age-old foundations;*
*you will be called Repairer of Broken Walls,*
*Restorer of Streets with Dwellings.*

Isaiah 58:1-12

Some people have abandoned prayer and fasting because they didn't seem to be getting the desired results. But can the problem lie with God? Is it not our own attitude that is at fault? When you pray and fast and do not experience a breakthrough, there is something in your life that needs to be dealt with. Maybe your motives for fasting were wrong in the first place.

The people of Isaiah's time also fasted without result. They were offended and asked God for an explanation. Why was He not answering His people and honoring their sacrifices? In many ways, they can be compared to the people around us today.

*For day after day they seek me out;*
*they seem eager to know my ways,*                     Verse 2

As a people, we do want to know the will of God for our lives.

*As if they were a nation that does what is right*
                                                           Verse 2

Many countries, like the United States, were founded upon godly principles.

*And has not forsaken the commands of its God.*
                                                           Verse 2

Despite the infiltration of immorality and debauchery into the very heart of our modern culture, a majority of people are still very religious.

*They ask me for just decisions .*              Verse 2

We are very concerned with social justice. We are against abortion, pornography, euthanasia and the spread of illegal drugs. We readily respond to pleas to demonstrate our feelings on these important subjects. We want to see positive changes in our society.

*And seem eager for God to come near them.*
                                                           Verse 2

The people of Isaiah's day even took *"delight in approaching God"* (KJV). They had a lot going for them, a lot to commend. But, if all this is true, why was God not hearing their prayers? Why was their fasting producing no visible results? They asked God the same question.

*'Why have we fasted,' they say,*
*'and you have not seen it? '*

*'Why have we humbled ourselves,*
*and you have not noticed?'*                    Verse 3

This sounds like a good question to me. These people thought they were serving God. They thought they were believing His Word. They were continuing their religious traditions and working for social justice in their day. Yet, when they quoted the promises and exercised their faith, nothing happened.

---

**When you pray and fast and do not experience a breakthrough, there is something in your life that needs to be dealt with.**

---

The answer God gave them may surprise some Christians:

*'Yet on the day of your fasting, you do as you please*
*and exploit all your workers.*
*Your fasting ends in quarreling and strife,*
*and in striking each other with wicked fists.*
*You cannot fast as you do today*
*and expect your voice to be heard on high.*
*Is this the kind of fast I have chosen?'*      Verses 3-5

If the people of Isaiah's day were getting nowhere spiritually because they were pleasure seekers, we are really in trouble in the closing years of the twentieth century. A great percentage of our time, our effort, and our money are now spent for things that bring us pleasure.

If the people of Isaiah's day were getting nowhere spiritually because they were too wrapped up in their jobs, we are really in trouble in the closing years of the twentieth century. To most of us, nothing is more important than our jobs — NOTHING.

Pleasure and job are the two reasons most Christians have for not fasting. We have many "more important" things to do. Fasting is simply not in the schedule. There is no time for it. And this attitude is preventing many from seeing an answer to their prayers.

If God is not answering our prayers, something is wrong. Our attitude is wrong. Our concept of God is wrong. If we really put God first, He will never fail to put us first. But if we put Him third, He is not obligated to answer our every whim and fancy. If having fun is more important to us than having God's favor on our lives, there is not much hope for our spiritual future. If our jobs are more important to us than doing the will of God, we are in serious trouble.

There are more serious reasons for unanswered prayer, as there were in Isaiah's time:

> *Behold, ye fast for strife and debate, and to smite with the fist of wickedness: ye shall not fast as ye do this day, to make your voice to be heard on high. Is it such a fast that I have chosen?*          Verses 4-5 KJV

Those who fasted actually had an evil purpose in doing so. God declared that this was not the fast He had chosen.

*Is it only for bowing one's head like a reed*
*and for lying on sackcloth and ashes?*
*Is that what you call a fast, a day acceptable to the*
*LORD?*                                                      Verse 5

The Pharisees made much of their fasting by putting on
sackcloth and ashes, ostensibly as an act of contrition, but
actually to make a show of their piety. Prayer and fasting
is not for the purpose of showing off. It is a very personal
act performed unto God, not unto men.

The fast which God has chosen is very different.

*Is not this the kind of fasting I have chosen:*
*to loose the chains of injustice*
*and untie the cords of the yoke,*
*to set the oppressed free and break every yoke?*
*Is it not to share your food with the hungry*
*and to provide the poor wanderer with shelter —*
*when you see the naked, to clothe him,*
*and not to turn away from your own flesh and blood?*
                                                      Verses 6-7

Our purpose for fasting is to *"loose the chains of injustice,"*
to *"untie the cords of the yoke,"* to *"set the oppressed free,"* and
to *"break every yoke."* This is the heart of God. When we
begin praying the heart of God and fasting for the desires
of the heart of God, we will see results. If we can only fast
for a new car or for a house, our motives are wrong and
we will be disappointed with the result of our sacrifice.

If you have been fasting and praying and have not received answers, carefully check your attitude. If your

heart is open, God will show you where you have erred. If you been discouraged to pray and fast by a lack of results in the past, **God is giving you a chance to return to biblical prayer and fasting** — which always brings the desired result.

# Chapter 4

## *The Recent Emphasis On Faith As a Cure-all*

*And without faith it is impossible to please God, because anyone who comes to him must believe that he exists and that he rewards those who earnestly seek him.*                                    Hebrews 11:6

Traditionally, prayer and fasting has been one of the strong points of evangelical, Pentecostal and Charismatic doctrine. Yet today even those groups have stopped fasting. Why do so few of our modern-day Charismatics fast? Why have a majority of the evangelicals and Pentecostals stopped fasting?

For some of our Spirit-filled brothers, it was the discovery of the "word of faith" and its operation that led to the abandonment of prayer and fasting. When believers discovered that by simply exercising the promise of God they could move heaven, they decided that prayer and fasting were no longer necessary. Nothing could be further from the truth. It is a sensitivity to the Spirit of God that gives us power to exercise the Word of God properly.

"Just speak the Word," many say, "and anything is possible." If that is true, why have so many of those who proclaimed that truth stopped experiencing miracles in their personal lives and in their ministries? When they stopped seeking God in prayer and fasting, they started an immediate spiritual decline. They were on their way down; they just didn't realize it at the time.

Some have turned to prophecy as a substitute for miracles. Prophecy was not meant to be a substitute for miracles. Prophecy is wonderful, and the Bible tells us not to despise prophecy (1 Thessalonians 5:20). But prophecy without the supernatural is not biblical prophecy at all. We need the demonstration of the power of God in our midst.

To maintain the crowds in their churches or ministries when the miracles are gone, most people turn to gimmicks. Slowly, they trust more and more in the world for guidance. Many don't even realize what is happening to them — until it is too late.

Emphasis on faith and the need to exercise it is not a bad thing. The Bible is clear: *"Without faith it is impossible to please God."* Faith pleases God, but faith cannot bring you everything that you need. The key phrase here is *"those who earnestly seek Him."* Faith depends upon a strong relationship to God. A strong relationship to God can be built by *"seek[ing] Him."* And prayer and fasting is the best way to seek Him.

Those who emphasize super-faith say that when things don't go well for you, it is because you don't have enough faith. Because of this, the bookstores are full of new titles on faith. This leads to other conclusions. If all you need is more faith, why pray? Prayer is hard work. Why do it — if it is not necessary? If all we need is faith, why fast? Fasting is not enjoyable to the flesh. Why do it — if we don't have to? If we are saved and on our way to heaven, why fast? Why not just enjoy this Christian life? Why not just rejoice in what we have?

That all sounds good, but what we are not told is that in order to maintain a strong faith and in order to stay saved and to be effective in the Kingdom of God, we must maintain a strong relationship with our heavenly Father; and this is done through prayer and fasting.

> *"O unbelieving and perverse generation," Jesus replied, "how long shall I stay with you? How long shall I put up with you? Bring the boy here to me."*
> Matthew 17:17

When the disciples of Jesus brought a child to Him whom they were unable to help, He called them an *"unbelieving and perverse generation"* and asked them, *"How long shall I stay with you? How long shall I put up with you?"* How could Jesus do that to His disciples? These men had left everything to follow Him. They had made great sacrifices to be at His side.

What He did next helps to explain His words. He called for the child. Then He *"rebuked the demon."* The result was that *"it came out of the boy, and he was healed from that moment."* (Verse 18). It was so easy for Jesus. Just a word from Him was sufficient. He had power and authority. No demon could stand against Him. When He spoke demons obeyed. He expected His disciples to have this same power. When they didn't, He chastened them.

Is it easy for us to deliver epileptics today? It can be — if we are prepared. But most of us are not. We struggle with the situations of life: the problems in the work place, the tensions in the home, the difficulties in the church and, most of all, the battles we face with our own character. We quote promises and exercise faith, but nothing seems to change. Jesus wanted to show us that it can all be so easy — if we are prepared, as He was prepared.

No wonder the church is weak! No wonder the church is not expecting miracles! The church has stopped seeking God in prayer and fasting.

If you have faith like a mustard seed, Jesus said, you can speak to mountains to move, and they will obey you. Faith makes the impossible possible. It brings into the realm of reality what can otherwise only be dreamed of. Faith goes beyond what the natural eye sees. According to Hebrews: *"Faith is the substance of things hoped for, the evidence of things not seen"* (Hebrews 11:1 KJV). Those who have no faith cannot please God. That is a principle.

God can only be perceived by faith. His creation of the world and everything that is in it can be understood only by faith. His Word can be accepted only by faith. So Jesus said that if we have just a little faith we can move mountains. Faith changes everything. Faith makes everything possible. Faith unlocks every door and opens to the believer every opportunity.

Without prayer and fasting, however, our faith cannot function. Some miracles will never happen without prayer and fasting. Some circumstances will never change without prayer and fasting. Some situations will never be reversed without prayer and fasting. Prayer and fasting sharpen your expectancy so that when you ask you expect to receive.

---

Prayer and fasting sharpen your expectancy so that when you ask you expect to receive.

---

The promises of God are conditional upon our living the life He has outlined for us. For instance, God delights to feed His children. David said:

> *I was young and now I am old, yet I have never seen the righteous forsaken or their children begging bread.*
> Psalms 37:25

This doesn't mean that we do nothing and receive everything as we have heard many teaching over the past ten or fifteen years. "Just speak the word in faith," we have heard over and over. That is not a wrong teaching; but it is also not a complete teaching. Many people have exercised their faith for big cars, for big houses, and for fancy restaurants, and their soul is leaner today than it was ten years ago. They get less answers to prayer now than before. They may be living like Texans, but they don't have the power of God in their lives.

If you are one of those who are eager to overcome error and to know truth and have been concerned about the deceptive teaching of faith as a cure-all, please read the remaining pages of this book very carefully. God wants to teach you the balanced Word. He wants to make your faith effective. He wants to lead you into a life of communion with Him that will bring you the victories you have so desired.

# Chapter 5

## *The Prevalence of the Spirit of Gluttony*

*Brethren, be followers together of me, and mark them which walk so as ye have us for an ensample. (For many walk, of whom I have told you often, and now tell you even weeping, that they are the enemies of the cross of Christ: Whose end is destruction, whose God is their belly, and whose glory is in their shame, who mind earthly things.)* Philippians 3:17-19 KJV

There is a new god in the land. His name is FOOD. He was already at work in Paul's day. He is also known as the BELLY god. FOOD is one of the most powerful gods at work in our society. In many places, he rules supreme.

The sad thing is that FOOD rules many Christians. Many of us work, not to the glory of God or for the good of His Kingdom, but for *daily bread*. If Jesus Himself appeared to us in the flesh and called us to forsake all and follow Him, most of us would consider it to be a trick of the Devil and would avoid obeying at any cost. Nothing is more important than our job, because it produces FOOD.

The best attended Christian activities these days are: banquets, breakfasts, picnics and barbecues. When we call for those who will travail for the purpose of God to be revealed and for revival for a city or a nation, we can count on our fingers those who show up. In order to assure people's attendance at church activities, we have to promise a Mexican feast, special Italian lasagna or spaghetti, or some similar FOOD.

Most of the well-attended conventions being conducted across the country advertise their good food. How many people would attend these activities if no food was served? How many would show up for several days of prayer and fasting?

Many churches now have to serve donuts and coffee in Sunday School and refreshments after Board Meeting to insure proper attendance. FOOD has become our idol.

At the same time we are worshiping at the altar of FOOD, we are saying to God, "God, we want to see your power and glory."

God is saying to us, "You are not really serious. You don't mean what you are saying. You are just playing with words."

Do we really want to see God's power and glory? Do we really want a new anointing upon our lives? Do we really want to see a spiritual breakthrough in our nations, in our governments, in our homes, in our marriages, in the lives of our children, and in our own personal experience with God?

Why is it that we have quoted the Word from Genesis to Revelation, and nothing is happening? Have we tried prayer and fasting? Perhaps our god, FOOD, has not permitted us to do that.

Some people will not attend certain churches because they don't let out early enough on Sunday morning. They must eat at the "accustomed" hour. Some people have God on a time clock. They offer Him two hours a week. If the service extends a few minutes over the allotted time, they get up and walk out. They leave Him because of FOOD. When 12:30 comes, their stomach begins to growl, and they simply can't keep their minds on the things of God any longer.

---

FOOD is one of the most powerful gods at work in our society. In many places, he rules supreme.

---

This is a far more serious matter than we might think. I am not trying to be funny. The Apostle Paul called such people *"enemies of the cross of Christ."*

FOOD is so important to us today. When men consider marriage, they look for a woman who is a good cook, not a woman who loves God. To these men, an ideal woman is one who will faithfully have a delicious meal ready for them when they get home from work.

Paul knew that there were more important things. He was determined to *"press toward the mark for the prize of the high calling of God in Christ Jesus"* (Philippians 3:14 KJV).

Concerning those whose god was BELLY, Paul predicted that their end would be *"destruction."* They were more concerned with *"earthly things"* than with the will of God for their lives.

Anytime the church ceases to embrace the godly practice of prayer and fasting, it begins an inexorable slide toward *"destruction."* Anytime the church gives in to the god, FOOD, its glory becomes *"shame."* Anytime the church is more concerned about *"earthly things"* than she is about spiritual things, she is headed for ruin. She cannot prevail under such circumstances. This is not my word. This is the eternal Word of God. Giving in to our appetites, or self-indulgence, is sin; and it separates us from the presence and blessing of God.

When God delivered His people from bondage in Egypt and sent them on their way to the Promised Land, occasionally they were tempted to go back — despite what they had suffered in Egypt. What could make people want to return to slavery?

> *We remember the fish we ate in Egypt at no cost —*
> *also the cucumbers, melons, leeks, onions and garlic.*
> Numbers 11:5

While some were remembering the amazing way in which God sent the plagues upon Egypt and the way He destroyed the Egyptian army in the Red Sea, others were thinking of what they had grown accustomed to eating around the fires in Goshen. They were not rejoicing about manna from Heaven. They were longing for leeks and cucumbers.

That may surprise some people, but it doesn't surprise me. I know Christians who can remember exactly what they had to eat at homecoming twenty years ago. They cannot remember who was saved in the last revival or when they last had a burden to pray for people in need. But they can remember who brought what to the church picnic.

Many people actually live by their stomachs. It is their clock. When they get hungry in the morning, they know it is time to get up. When they feel hungry later in the day, they know it is lunchtime. When they get hungry again, they get excited because they know it is quitting time. These people even dream about food. Are these people really Christians? Well, they still call themselves Christians. But they are unaware of the fact that a strange idol has taken control of their lives.

God has not ordained that we be ruled by our appetites. The Christian life means freedom from our appetites. When we are slaves to our appetites, we are carnally minded. And the carnal (*sinful*) mind is God's enemy.

> *The sinful mind is hostile to God. It does not submit to God's law, nor can it do so.* Romans 8:7

Being a Christian and being dominated by appetite are two incompatible things. The two are so contrary the one to the other that they cannot coexist. They do not go together.

Many have fallen into this deceit because of the popular belief that we simply must give special attention to food in

order to exist. I am glad that Jesus answered that for all
eternity, when He said:

> *Man shall not live by bread alone, but by every word*
> *that proceedeth out of the mouth of God.*
> Matthew 4:4 KJV

Jesus taught us to labor for lasting values, for that which
does not perish.

> *"Do not work for food that spoils, but for food that*
> *endures to eternal life, which the Son of Man will give*
> *you. On him God the Father has placed his seal of*
> *approval."*                                                                    John 6:27

FOOD is not a very good god. It perishes. When we eat
it, we feel satisfied for a very short time. How much better
it is to put our efforts into lasting things! And how sad it is
to lose the blessing of God for something so insignificant
and temporal as FOOD!

FOOD has become so important to some of us that we
are living for the invitation to visit the home of other
people to eat with them. When a week passes without
such an invitation, we get concerned and make it a matter
of prayer. We ask God to touch their hearts so they will
invite us. That's how important FOOD is to some people.
If you are consumed by such desires, hear the Word of
the Lord:

> *When you sit to dine with a ruler, note well what is*
> *before you, and put a knife to your throat if you are*

*given to gluttony. Do not crave his delicacies, for that
food is deceptive. Do not wear yourself out to get rich;
have the wisdom to show restraint.*

Proverbs 23:1-4

Gluttony leads to other sins. If you don't get control
over it, it will control you. *"Put a knife to your throat"*
doesn't mean commit suicide. It means to suppress your
appetites.

*"Have the wisdom to show restraint."* You think you know
how to handle life; but God knows so much better than
you; and He is telling you to get control over your natural
appetites before they get control over you.

Gluttony leads men to poverty.

*For drunkards and gluttons become poor, and
drowsiness clothes them in rags.*          Proverbs 23:21

According to the Bible, *"gluttons"* are in the same class
with *"drunkards."* And both of them will *"become poor."*
Yet, even in the church, the most popular occasions are
Thanksgiving, Christmas, Homecoming, the Annual Picnic and New Year's Eve — all occasions for special
feasting.

What does Thanksgiving mean to the average citizen
today? It means FOOD! Because of that many people in
America have stopped calling the day "Thanksgiving"
and started calling it "Turkey Day." That probably ex-
presses better what most Americans do on that day.

What does New Years mean to the average person today? It means special FOOD!

What does Sunday mean to a lot of people today? It means special FOOD!

No wonder we have lost the power of God! No wonder poverty has overtaken the church! No wonder the kingdom of darkness is advancing on every front!

Our churches are in crisis; our families are in crisis; our nation is in crisis; and we are crying out: "Oh God, raise up men and women who can touch You in prayer and bring revival to the nation." But we finish the prayer quickly because everyone is hungry and wants to eat before the food gets cold. Is it any wonder that our prayers are not prevailing?

James said of Elijah:

> *Elijah was a man just like us. He prayed earnestly that it would not rain, and it did not rain on the land for three and a half years. Again he prayed, and the heavens gave rain, and the earth produced its crops.*
>
> James 5:17-18

James was careful not to give us the impression that Elijah was some superhuman being. He was *"a man just like us."* He was just as human as any one of us. Yet his prayer prevailed. When he asked God to close the heavens, the heavens were closed. When he asked God for rain, it rained.

Did God just choose Elijah and sovereignly decide to favor him above others? I don't believe so. I believe that Elijah had power with God because he fasted and prayed, got control of his appetites, and developed a strong relationship with his heavenly Father.

It is true that God wants to feed His children; but He never intended for FOOD to dominate our lives. God gave us sex; but He intended for sex to be used within the confines of the marriage. God gave us plants; but He never intended for us to smoke them and inject their ingredients into our veins for false "highs." Everything has its purpose. We were not destined to be controlled by FOOD.

To many people, the most important thing to do on payday is go to the grocery store. They wouldn't miss it for anything. Some people are slaves to GRITS. Some serve the god SAUSAGE. Some are bound by ORANGE JUICE. When these people hear the word "fast," they are frightened. They think they might die if they fasted.

FOOD, for many, is like a security blanket. It comforts them and causes them not to be afraid. They develop a dependency on it.

Those who go through periods of depression go to the refrigerator often, every ten minutes or so, looking for something to soothe their frayed nerves. People who can't sleep at night sneak down to the refrigerator, hoping to find something there that will help them to rest. For some, their dependency on FOOD is just as serious as an alcohol or drug dependency for others. They have been tricked by the Enemy of their souls into making FOOD an idol. And Satan is delighted!

To these people, doing without food for even one day seems like a most horrible prospect. They cannot conceive of life without their idol. Taking away FOOD, for them, means taking away the joy of life. They look forward to mealtimes. What else is there to live for?

Many people know that they should fast and want to fast, but they can't. They don't know how to break the food habit. They don't know how to get their thoughts and their emotions under control long enough to seek God seriously. Satan is having a field day, diverting the attention of God's people away from Him.

I am shocked to see the millions of dollars that are spent to advertise California raisins. But the ads work. They make you hungry for raisins.

Ray Charles is effective for Diet Pepsi. He makes you want to drink one.

Some rock stars are paid millions of dollars for a single ad for FOOD. Those ads are an attack on your desire to seek God in prayer and fasting. They make FOOD look so real and so delicious you want to reach out and touch it — just like the AT&T slogan.

When you turn on the television today, you see what broadcasters have determined viewers want to see: scandals, sex, violence, and FOOD. (A cooking segment has recently become a regular evening news feature of a major Washington, D.C. station because that is what people want to hear.)

Many people are actually drunk on FOOD. They are under the influence of what they eat, and they need deliverance. As believers, we take pride in the fact that we are no longer addicted to drugs or alcohol. Yet many of us are even more addicted to FOOD and live for our stomachs.

When I first came to America many years ago, I was shocked by what I witnessed. Everywhere I went people were offering me food. In our country, it is impolite to refuse an offer of hospitality. So I ate what was set before me and drank enough Kool Aid to sink a battle ship. I thought of the words of Jesus:

> *For in the days before the flood, people were eating and drinking, marrying and giving in marriage, up to the day Noah entered the ark; and they knew nothing about what would happen until the flood came and took them all away. That is how it will be at the coming of the Son of Man.* Matthew 24:38-39

We show one another love by serving something good to eat. We share our favorite recipes with our favorite people. Most Christians are more familiar with the latest dessert fads than they are with the books of the Bible.

And pastors are not without blame in all of this. Sometimes pastors are the worst offenders. Many pastors have bellies that are several times the size they should be. It seems that some of them rush through their sermons so they can go on picnics. If pastors are gluttons, how can they care for the spiritual needs of the flock over which God has placed them? How can they help their members to be delivered from their bad habits? How can they give spiritual direction to others?

What good is a pastor who is unconcerned with the health and welfare of his congregation? God says:

> *If my people, who are called by my name, will humble themselves and pray and seek my face and turn from their wicked ways, then will I hear from heaven and will forgive their sin and will heal their land.*
> 2 Chronicles 7:14

Pastors, if banquets are more important to us than prayer and fasting we are in trouble.

Some preachers are tempted by every smell of food. They know what is being served in Red Lobster as they drive by, and they want to go in and enjoy some of it. They know what the special of the day is in the local restaurant — just by the smell. You never hear them say anymore, "I sense that God is in that place. Let's go in there and see what is happening." If the shepherds have strayed, is it any wonder that the sheep seem to be lost?

Pastors, let us arise and declare that the principle reason many Christians do not get answers to prayer is that they never fast. Let us declare that because FOOD has become a god in our society, abstaining from food is one of the surest ways of find God's perfect will for our lives. Let us be bold to make known that in these days of difficult family and personal relationships, **we simply will not make it without a dedication to a life of prayer and fasting.**

# Chapter 6

## *The Selfish Spirit of the Age*

*He that laboureth laboureth for himself; for his mouth craveth it of him.*                    Proverbs 16:26 KJV

Everything about our present orientation in our modern society is selfish. From the time they are old enough to learn, our children are being taught to look out for themselves. Our market economic system teaches us to look after our own interests. Instead of concern for our neighbors, as Jesus taught, our theme today is total self-reliance.

The church has been affected by this spirit of our time. This is one of the major reasons that Christians have stopped fasting. They are getting along fine. They are able to pay their bills and have a little left over. There is nothing for them to worry about. Why fast? When some tragedy strikes them, they are unprepared; by then it is usually too late to fast.

Who has a burden to fast for the nation? Who has a burden to fast for its leaders? Who has a burden to fast for the community? Who has a burden to fast for drug addicts? Who has a burden to fast for those who are sick and afflicted?

Some churches fast for new air conditioners and better pews so that they can be more comfortable during their short visits to the sanctuary. But their fasting goes no further than that.

The major concerns of churches today are for excellence in attendance, in program and in reputation:

Which church has the largest building?
Which church has the most attendance on
Sunday morning?
Which church has the broadest program?
Which church can raise the most money?

No wonder the Devil is not disturbed by what he sees! Churches with such a limited vision will never endanger his kingdom. He is not afraid of numbers or programs or money. It is still the power of God that puts him to flight. Satan fears the power that is realized through prayer and fasting.

Even those who receive the anointing of the Spirit today want to use that anointing for themselves and their own needs and desires. The next time they pray, they keep asking:

*Why can't I get anything from God?*
*Why can't I get anything from God?*

At the same time, God is asking:

*Why can't I get anything from YOU?*
*Why can't I get anything from YOU?*

God wants us to *"undo the heavy burdens."* He wants us to *"set the captives free."* If we could just forget ourselves for a few minutes and seek the mind of the Lord, we would see the greatness He has prepared for us. If we could get to know what is in the heart of the Father, prayer and fasting would take on a whole new meaning for us.

---

No wonder the Devil is not disturbed by what he sees. Churches with these visions will never endanger his kingdom.

---

We are even selfish in our worship. Most people don't go to church to worship God. They go to church to present their wish list. And most Christians will not attend prayer meetings, where they would have the opportunity to seek God more. They have no time for that.

It seems that the two most dreaded things in the Western church today are systematic Bible study and prayer and fasting. Instead of benefits, we treat them as our enemies.

Ministers who visit third-world countries come back impressed by several things they have witnessed: the poverty-stricken state of that nation, the sincerity of the people of that nation and the commitment of the believers of that nation to the Lord, to His Church and to His people. Their routine of living includes regular prayer and fasting.

What has happened to the Christian commitment of those of us in the more developed nations? If Jesus appeared today in the flesh and called many of us to serve Him, the first thing we would ask Him would be how much the job paid, what job security was offered, and what the benefits were. That is how selfish we have become.

If our interest in earning money were for the purpose of promoting the Kingdom of God, that would be one thing. Most Christians, however, are interested in money only for the pleasures and comforts it brings them. Many Christians are even robbing God by giving less than is due, so that they can enjoy more of the "good life." When they were poor, they faithfully tithed; but now that God has prospered them, they never have enough. They take the tithe and use it for more luxuries. They think God owes them a good time in life. They see everything as being for their pleasure.

Solomon knew such people. He said: *"He that laboureth laboureth for himself."* That is why the Enemy is able to use the argument: *You worked hard. Now enjoy it.*

The problem is that when you are selfishly oriented, there never seems to be enough. Jesus told of a young man who was prospering. He was so blessed that he had a major decision to make concerning the expansion of his business.

*And he told them this parable: "The ground of a certain rich man produced a good crop. He thought to himself, 'What shall I do? I have no place to store my crops.' "Then he said, 'This is what I'll do. I will tear down my barns and build bigger ones, and there I will store all my grain and my goods. And I'll say to myself, "You have plenty of good things laid up for many years. Take life easy; eat, drink and be merry." But God said to him, 'You fool! This very night your life will be demanded from you. Then who will get what you have prepared for yourself?' "This is how it will be with anyone who stores up things for himself but is not rich toward God."* Luke 12:16-21

This man fell for Satan's line. He had worked hard. He deserved everything that he had received. He was already "rich" when the parable started. Now he was rich beyond his wildest dreams. What would he do with his new-found wealth? He decided to flaunt his good fortune and to lavish his wealth upon himself. Because he laid up treasure for himself but was not rich toward God, his end was sad. That very night his soul was required of him. Isn't it ironic that selfishness robs us of the very blessings we seek in being selfish in the first place?

There are two very important lessons for us to learn here. The first is that riches never satisfy.

*All man's efforts are for his mouth, yet his appetite is never satisfied.* Ecclesiastes 6:7

The second lesson we must learn from this parable is that when God prospers us it is not for us to turn away from Him and give ourselves to things. When He prospers us it is not so that we can spend more time with our possessions and neglect Him. When He prospers us it is not so that we can afford to eat better and develop uncontrollable appetites that prevent us from seeking the God that formed us.

God prospers us so that the vision for His Kingdom can be established and so that we can be a blessing to others, not so that we can be overcome with the cares of life. One of the sins of Noah's day was *"they were eating and drinking"* (Matthew 24:38 KJV). In spite of that, *"eating and drinking"* to some people is what prosperity is all about. The prosperity that God gives is much deeper and richer.

That presumptuous rich farmer in Luke 12 had a lot to learn.

> '*And I'll say to myself, "You have plenty of good things laid up for many years. Take life easy; eat, drink and be merry."* '                    Luke 12:19

How smug! He thought he had life all figured out. He thought he knew it all. What a great surprise he had coming!

Selfish people never pray and fast. Prayer and fasting take time, time which you cannot spend on something else. Prayer and fasting take effort, effort that you won't be able to spend on some other pursuit. That's what turns most Christians off to prayer and fasting. Time is so short anyway. Prayer and fasting simply don't rate high on their list of priorities.

When there are problems and critical decisions that face an entire congregation and we need everyone to join together in a period of prayer and fasting, you can count on many people being "too busy" to do their part. They have other, "more important" things to do.

When they have a need that touches them personally, they want everyone to join with them in prayer. Have our prayers all become selfish in nature? Is it all *"me," "my," "mine"* and *"myself"*?

No wonder God doesn't answer! We are way off base when we pray this way. Our attitudes are all wrong. Our motivation is all wrong. Our timing is all wrong. Our priorities are all wrong.

Some people still fast — but only for a selfish purpose. They want to lose weight. However, that is not the purpose of fasting; and fasting just to lose weight will not bring you the spiritual benefits the Bible promises to those who learn this secret and exercise it faithfully.

Television advertising makes you selfish. It makes you want many things that will not help you at all and many other things that will be detrimental to your physical and spiritual well-being.

Television has made your children selfish. They want the things they see on television — whether they are good for them or not. Worse, your children are taking their role models from the television programs they watch. You may make excuses for them: *This is just a passing fad.* The truth is that Satan has an intense campaign to win the soul of your children, to make them totally selfish.

Many of them have made idols of the rock stars they see on television. They are no longer imitating Daniel or Deborah, but Michael and Madonna. The posters hanging in their bedrooms let you know where their heart is.

God has blessed my wife and me with two beautiful girls, Anna-Kissel and Damaris Joy, and I thank God for them. I try to teach them to honor the presence of God and to respect the house of God. David said:

> *I rejoiced with those who said to me, "Let us go to the house of the Lord."* Psalms 122:1

I want my daughters to grow up with the blessing of God upon their lives.

If you are totally selfish and are living a life of selfishness, it is impossible to teach your children something different. If your job, your car and your house take precedence over God and His house, your children will imitate you.

God is interested in your job, your car and the house in which you live. But He is interested in far more than those three things. Why is it that most every believer spends so much time believing God for these three things when there is so much more?

Get your priorities sorted out. Don't take your cue from this selfish world system but from the eternal Word of God. When you do, **you will find prayer and fasting and seeking the face of God very high on your list of priorities.**

# Chapter 7

## *The Lack of Teaching on the Subject of PRAYER AND FASTING*

*My people are destroyed from lack of knowledge.*
Hosea 4:6

Aside from these obvious reasons that many Christians have abandoned the custom of prayer and fasting, many simply have never been taught, especially among new converts. Older Christians know about prayer and fasting because it was more commonly taught and practiced years ago. Today it is a neglected doctrine of the Church.

Many churches actually denounce fasting. Some teach that it was a pagan practice that has no place in Christianity. As such, it is considered to be heresy. Others teach that fasting was only for a former time. The leaders of these churches never fast and they also never experience miracles.

If fasting were not important and biblical, Jesus would never have fasted. He is our example; and He did it.

---

**If fasting were not important and biblical, Jesus would never have fasted.**

---

Among important Bible subjects, fasting has to take its place near the top. There is just as much teaching about prayer and fasting in the Bible as there is about many of the more commonly taught doctrines.

Having lost sight of its importance and what it will do for us, few Bible teachers are taking time to lay the biblical foundations necessary in every new believer to a life of dedication to prayer and fasting. As a result, some people are still unaware that fasting is in the Bible.

---

**There is just as much teaching about prayer and fasting in the Bible as there is about many of the more commonly taught doctrines.**

---

There is a more sinister reason that many pastors no longer teach prayer and fasting. It is not a very popular subject. It is not something the ear delights to hear.

Therefore, it is shunned as "too controversial." Some would rather teach what people want to hear than what they need to hear.

Congregations are increasingly better educated; and fasting, to some well-educated people, seems absurd and illogical. How could abstinence from food have so many benefits? It doesn't seem to make scientific sense. But doesn't most of God's Word seem absurd to the natural mind? Aren't God's ways strange to all of us?

I have two doctorates, one in theology and one in philosophy and a background in electronic engineering. But I still know that prayer and fasting works and has been ordained of God for a divine purpose. Whether others understand this or not, I personally am determined to do God's will. **I am determined, for the sake of my soul and that of my family members and for my ministry to the world, to live a life dedicated to prayer and fasting and to teach others the benefits of doing the same.**

# Part III

# Why We Should Pray and Fast (Purpose)

## *Introduction to Part III*

Many of those who still fast regard fasting as a convenient way of getting God to give them things they want; and that's the only reason they ever fast. They never fast long. They never do much praying with their fasting. They never fast joyfully. Fasting, for them, is just a means of twisting God's arm to get what they want. Why should we fast? What is the PURPOSE?

# Chapter 8

## *The Need to Crucify the Flesh*

*What causes fights and quarrels among you? Don't they come from your desires that battle within you? You want something but don't get it. You kill and covet, but you cannot have what you want. You quarrel and fight. You do not have, because you do not ask God. When you ask, you do not receive, because you ask with wrong motives, that you may spend what you get on your pleasures.* James 4:1-3

Fasting is not a tool to twist the arm of God so that He will give you exactly what you want. Fasting has a spiritual purpose, and that purpose is to get your flesh out of the way so that the Spirit of God can move in your life. Fasting removes the barriers to communication with God and allows the spirit man to commune directly with the heavenly Father — without disturbance. When a person makes a determination to fast, they are making a determination to remove the obstacles in their life to total submission to the will of God.

No wonder Satan is determined to eradicate this practice! Fasting tears down his strongholds. Fasting clears the way for our victory. He will do anything to prevent that.

And Satan wants you to be poor, to give free rein to your appetites — until they consume you. The food industry, the illegal drug industry, and the entertainment industry have much in common. They are all pandering to the runaway appetites of our society. Much of the poverty of our ghettos and projects is a direct result of this almost total loss of control.

Most of us who live comfortably in the prosperous nations have problems with prayer and fasting because everything around us is designed to appeal to our flesh and its carnal desires. But when we seek the face of God through prayer and fasting, we push the flesh aside, denying the appetites the control they seek over us, and allowing our spirit man, who desires God, to develop a strong relationship with the heavenly Father.

Man is a triune being made up of body, soul and spirit. It is the spirit that came from God and longs to be reunited with God. Given the opportunity, the spirit will reach out to God and communicate with Him.

These three parts of the person, however, compete for influence. Your spirit can influence your soul, and your soul can influence your flesh. If you are in tune spiritually with God, your soul has no choice but to delight in the decisions of your spiritual life.

Your flesh submits to the authority of your soul. When the angel Gabriel appeared to Mary, she responded:

*"My soul glorifies the Lord and my spirit rejoices in God my Savior."*                    Luke 1:46-47

If your soul is magnifying the Lord, your flesh will bow in submission. If your flesh has risen to authority in your life, however, it will struggle with your spirit for dominance, and the soul will obey the lusts of the flesh. Fasting sets your spirit free to worship and serve God.

Fasting is not a tool to twist the arm of God so that He will give you exactly what you want. Fasting has a spiritual purpose, and that purpose is to get your flesh out of the way so that the Spirit of God can move in your life.

When we resist the Spirit of God, we open ourselves up to the evil influence of Satan. Each of us then — men, women, boys, and girls — are either controlled by the Holy Spirit or by Satan. That thought alone should drive every believer to prayer and fasting.

Fasting enables you to break the hold of the flesh and bring your appetites into control. It places you in submission to the Spirit of God. When this happens, you get answers to your prayers.

> *From whence come wars and fightings among you?*
> *come they not hence, even of your lusts that war in*
> *your members? Ye lust, and have not: ye kill, and*
> *desire to have, and cannot obtain: ye fight and war, yet*
> *ye have not, because ye ask not. Ye ask, and receive*
> *not, because ye ask amiss, that ye may consume it*
> *upon your lusts.*                           James 4:1-3 KJV

James gives two reasons that our prayers go unanswered. The first is that we simply don't ask. The second is that we ask *"amiss,"* we ask with wrong motives, we ask with fleshly desires, we ask with carnal intent — *"to consume it upon your lusts."*

Many of us are guilty of taking the blessings of God and consuming them upon our own lusts. Should we wonder why we don't get an immediate answer the next time?

If you constantly live and work for the flesh, you will produce the works of the flesh and death. If, however, you live and work in agreement with the Spirit of God, you produce life. This is why your flesh resists walking in the Spirit.

Your flesh resists anything that will bring it into subjection. Your flesh doesn't want to fast. You must insist or be doomed to be forever controlled by the flesh and the devil. Because this is so, the flesh will use every imaginable excuse to keep you from fasting. A few of the more common ones are:

> *You are not ready to fast.*
> *Now is not the best time.*

*You don't have time to really seek the face of God, so
you might as well wait for another opportunity.
You might offend other members of your family.*

When you want to fast and draw near to God, expect
the enemy of your soul to fight in every way possible to
prevent it. He doesn't want you to fast. At the very moment you decide to fast, he will present you with some ir-
resistable invitation to eat out. He will present you with a
well-done food advertisement. He will cause you to remember all your favorite foods. He will bring up obstacles
that you never imagined.

The God that we serve is the same God who sent manna
in the wilderness. He fed multitudes with a few loaves
and fishes. When He came to earth as a man, He could
have easily turned stones into bread to satisfy His hunger;
but He refused. He was determined to submit the flesh of
Jesus of Nazareth, the man, to His heavenly Father so that
He could have the power of God in His life. When His
period of prayer and fasting was ended, Jesus was
launched forth into a mighty ministry of deliverance and
miracles. That same power is waiting for each of us who
will dare to believe God and obey.

When your prayers are influenced by the flesh, they are
not proper prayers. James knew believers who were asking "amiss." Their motives were not good. They were
asking for selfish reasons. The Father, in love and mercy,
had to refuse their requests. He knows what is good for us.
He knows what we can handle; and He wants all the
glory. When the flesh intends to glory in the goodness of

God, God is forced to withhold His blessing. He cannot give the flesh any reason to glory.

For example, God cannot further bless many people on their jobs because if He did, they would take all the credit for the things He does. He wants all the glory. Daniel said: *"Wisdom and might are His"* (Daniel 2:20 KJV). God wants all the glory. The flesh must be crucified.

Get your flesh crucified so that God can get the glory in your life. If you can get your flesh out of the way, your steps can be *"ordered by the Lord"* (Psalm 37:23 KJV). If you can get your flesh out of the way, the Spirit can have full liberty to do what He desires in and through you. If you can get your flesh out of the way, you will have more clarity and a greater sensitivity in the Spirit what to ask for and you will receive the answer.

When we are dominated by the flesh, we don't even know what to pray for. We think we know what we need. But we are so much like little children. When we get closer to God through prayer and fasting, we begin to realize what we REALLY need. God knows better than us what we need. He can show us the priorities. He can also show us exactly how to go about receiving what we need.

David became the anointed king of Israel because he learned the secret of getting his flesh out of the way so that God could work in him. He said:

> My *knees are weak through fasting; and my flesh faileth of fatness.*                Psalms 109:24 KJV

David had weak knees from fasting, but it gave him a strong spirit. He brought his flesh into subjection. He waited in the presence of God, in prayer and fasting, until God anointed him to do exploits.

Why is it that we only fast when we have a problem? Why is it that we only spend time in prayer when we are in crisis? God is not pleased with this.

When we walk in faith and don't see any answer, I believe it is because there are many small impediments in our lives that need to be removed.

If we can discipline the body, our spirits will become useful instruments to God. Paul learned that lesson.

> *But I keep under my body, and bring it into subjection: lest that by any means, when I have preached to others, I myself should be a castaway.*
> 1 Corinthians 9:27 KJV

Fasting means that you are determined to walk from victory to victory. Fasting builds up your faith to accomplish it. Fasting removes the weaknesses in your life and leaves you strong to face life's battles. Paul stayed in the presence of God until he received the answer he needed.

> *Casting down imaginations, and every high thing that exalteth itself against the knowledge of God, and bringing into captivity every thought to the obedience of Christ;*
> 2 Corinthians 10:5 KJV

Fasting helps us to cast down those *"imaginations"* and all those *"high thing[s]"* that exalt themselves *"against the knowledge of God."* Fasting helps us to bring every thought into captivity to the obedience of Christ, as nothing else can. Fasting enables you to conquer the evil thoughts of your carnal mind.

Paul taught about experiences in prayer which few people have these days.

> *And pray in the Spirit on all occasions with all kinds of prayers and requests. With this in mind, be alert and always keep on praying for all the saints.*
>
> Ephesians 6:18

How do you pray *"all kinds of prayers"*? In other words, we should employ every method available to us in prayer. Many of us have been taught only one method of prayer. The method most people know is the "anguish" method. By that I mean that they only call on God in extreme emergencies, when they are in deep trouble. Those who go no further in their prayer life never learn how to praise God effectively. Yet, Jesus taught us that the very first thing we are to do in prayer is to give Him glory and the honor He deserves.

Many people take their long wish list into their period of prayer and fasting. They never wait on God for His wisdom, His knowledge, and His understanding. They are too busy asking Him for things.

If we are still in the "what-can-I-get" mode, we are still carnal, not spiritual at all. God is not looking for opportunists. He is looking for people who love and appreciate Him and want to build a relationship with Him just because they love Him, not because of what they can get in return. What we can get is just a benefit of the relationship we can build with our Father.

It is not wrong to get things from God. There are many things we need and He wants to supply. But the Spirit of Christ is not the Spirit of getting. It is the Spirit of giving. For this reason the Scriptures declare:

*God loves a cheerful giver.* 2 Corinthians 9:7

Before we start thinking about what we need from God, there are some things we can give to Him. Start by giving Him your heart, then give Him your praise, then give Him your time, etc.

*Pray continually.* 1 Thessalonians 5:17

Prayer means thinking with someone. When we say, "I am praying for you, we mean "I am agreeing with you. I am thinking with you." So when we pray, we think or reason with God.

Paul meant: "Don't stop praying. Don't stop thinking with God. Develop a life-style of praying."

Prayer is not always easy and praying always is not easy. Some people pray for just a few minutes and they have nothing more to say. If that is the case in your life it might be because you don't know the Word of God. His Word reveals His heart. It reveals what is important to Him. It reveals what grieves Him and what brings Him joy.

Some prayers are not prayers at all but complaints to God. That type of prayer cannot please Him. As you learn His Word, you will learn what pleases Him.

One of the worst aspects of the flesh is pride. Pride will take you straight into the arms of Satan, while a broken and humble spirit will take you straight into the arms of God. Fasting destroys pride, something that every one of us must struggle with at regular intervals in our lives. Fasting produces a humility of spirit. It makes you teachable. How greatly we need this particular benefit of fasting these days!

One thing is sure: Fasting will never take you down. When you develop a regular habit of fasting, you can only go upward spiritually.

Your flesh will complain. It will say that it is dying, that it is becoming ugly, that it is sick and weak. Don't give in to the flesh. Submit to the Spirit of God. You want the flesh to die. You will never be sorry that you crucified the flesh. The promise of the Scriptures is:

> *The mind of sinful man is death, but the mind controlled by the Spirit is life and peace;*     Romans 8:6

**Use prayer and fasting as the tool to deal flesh a deathblow.**

# Chapter 9

## *The Need to Hear the Voice of God*

*That servant who knows his master's will and does not get ready or does not do what his master wants will be beaten with many blows.*     Luke 12:47

Because Christ is our Lord and Savior and because we are totally dependent on Him, it is of the utmost importance that we know His will at any given time. This is the area where many Christians fail. To know the will of God it is necessary to live close to Him and to hear His voice.

Prayer and fasting makes you sensitive to the voice of the Lord. It enables you to hear Him above the din of other voices around you. What could be more important?

Because they have stopped fasting, many Christians have stopped hearing the voice of God and have resorted to setting out "fleeces" in an attempt to know the will of

God for their lives. They are no longer sure that God will hear their prayer and answer in a personal way. So, they set three signs: One means YES; the second means NO; and the third means WAIT. What a shame that God's children are no longer expecting to hear His voice!

If you have a child who comes to you and asks you for something and you can only respond, "Wait," that child will become impatient and go ahead and tamper with whatever he was told not to do at the moment. God wants to give His people specific and detailed answers to prayer, not just tell them to wait.

---

Prayer and fasting makes you sensitive to the voice of the Lord. It enables you to hear Him above the din of other voices around you. What could be more important?

---

If you tell your pre-teen son that you want to give him a car but that he must wait, that will weigh on his mind. He will anxiously await the day that you are away and he can take the keys to the car and take a little spin. The results may be disastrous. Most of us know better than to do that. When our pre-teens ask to drive, we say, "NO" —because we love them and we know what they can handle. When he becomes of age and demonstrates maturity and responsibility, the NO is lifted and becomes YES.

God knows what we can handle. He knows what's good for us. He knows what we will do with what He gives us. He doesn't have to answer in vague terms. His answers are specific and to the point.

Because they no longer hear the voice of God clearly, many of God's children are acting like immature pre-teens and getting themselves into trouble in the process. It is time to grow up and act like adult believers.

Every decision that we make should be inspired by God. Every move that we make should be ordained by Him. If our decisions and our moves are not inspired by God and in accordance with His will for our lives, we have no guarantee of success in what we do.

God is not trying to hide His will or to make it some mystery that is difficult to discover. He just wants to be able to communicate with you anytime what it is He wants for you. He wants you to seek Him.

> *But SEEK first his kingdom and his righteousness, and all these things will be given to you as well.*
> Matthew 6:33

> *Ask and it will be given to you; SEEK and you will find; knock and the door will be opened to you.*
> Matthew 7:7

> *God did this so that men would SEEK him and perhaps reach out for him and find him, though he is not far from each one of us.*     Acts 17:27

> *If ye then be risen with Christ, SEEK those things which are above, where Christ sitteth on the right hand of God.*     Colossians 3:1 KJV

*SEEK The Lord while he may be found; call on him
while he is near.*                                    Isaiah 55:6

When we seek the Lord, He promises to be found of us.

*You will SEEK me and find me when you seek me
with all your heart.*                              Jeremiah 29:13

Seeking the Lord and fasting also go together. It is difficult to seek the Lord *"with all your heart"* when you have a
full stomach. We desire to hear from God, but the flesh
wants to do its own thing. The flesh tells us to get comfortable.

*Change into something more comfortable!*
*Turn on the air-conditioner!*
*Get a cool drink from the refrigerator and something*
*to snack on!*
*Lie down on the couch!*
*Now, relax!*

And, before long, we are snoring and all thoughts of
seeking God are lost. It is amazing how many people
sleep in church. They eat before they go. The pews are
very comfortable. It is a little too warm because of the
crowd. The music is soothing. And, before long, they are
sound asleep.

Another reason that people sleep in church is because of
the atmosphere of peace and power that prevails in God's
house. Some who can't sleep well at home can sleep in
church. But that doesn't make it right. When you sleep in

church, you miss what God wants to do in your spirit at that moment. When you sleep in church you are robbing yourself of the blessings, both spiritual and physical, that God wants to give you. Fasting can cure that problem.

Those who never fast rarely see visions. They rarely have spiritual dreams. Overeating gives us nightmares. We dream about everything else except that which glorifies God.

When we fast and wait in the presence of God, He will speak to us in many different ways. He will put a word in our spirit. He will give us a vision or a dream. He speaks to us through circumstances, through nature, through a live experience or through preaching. Don't stop fasting until you have heard from God.

When I fast, I expect to hear from God. I expect Him to reveal Himself to me in a greater way. I expect to receive the specific instruction I need for my personal life and for my ministry. I expect Him to correct me in the areas where I am lacking. I expect Him to show me things about the future. And He never fails me.

It is not wrong to expect answers to your prayers. When I talk to God, I expect Him to respond. I know that He hears me, and I know that He will answer me. It is not wrong to expect to hear from God. He is anxiously waiting to reveal many things to us — if we will only dedicate ourselves to a time of seeking Him.

Knowing the will of God is the greatest struggle most Christians face in life:

> *Is it God's will for me to get married?*
> *Is this the right person for me?*
> *Lord, I want to know your will.*

*Is it God's will for me to go into business?*
*Or should I go into the ministry?*

These are important questions. Knowing and obeying God's will for our lives means the difference between success and failure. We desperately need to know His perfect will for today. We could avoid so many of the tragedies of life and be so blessed if we were more conscious of what God wanted.

Most decisions are made in Western society, be they political, social, spiritual, economical or educational, around a dining room table. Imagine the impact we could make if all our plans were made around dedicated prayer and fasting!

The only way to really know God's will is to get flesh pushed aside long enough to hear His voice and to discover His heart. **That, in itself, is sufficient reason for concerted prayer and fasting.**

# Chapter 10

## *The Need for Power*

*Then Jesus was led by the Spirit into the desert to be tempted by the devil. After fasting forty days and forty nights, he was hungry.* Matthew 4:1-2

Jesus is our example. He was *"led by the Spirit into the desert."* There He fasted *"forty days and forty nights."* He didn't go there to be seen of men. He didn't go there to fulfill some tradition of his fathers. He went there to get the power of God in His life; and when He came forth from that solitary place, no enemy could stand against Him. He was powerful.

*How God anointed Jesus of Nazareth with the Holy Spirit and power, and how he went around doing*

*good and healing all who were under the power of the
devil, because God was with him.*    Acts 10:38

When Jesus returned to the synagogue in Nazareth, He
was accorded the honor of a visitor and was given the
privilege of reading the Scriptures in public. The book
was given to Him, and He read from Isaiah:

*The Spirit of the Lord is on me, because he has
anointed me to preach good news to the poor. He has
sent me to proclaim freedom for the prisoners and
recovery of sight for the blind, to release the oppressed,
to proclaim the year of the Lord's favor.*
                                    Luke 4:18-19

When He had finished the reading, Jesus said to the
congregation: *"This day is this scripture fulfilled in your ears"*
(Luke 4:21 KJV). Waiting upon God the Father in prayer
and fasting had placed a special anointing upon the life of
Jesus, and that special anointing enabled Him to do the
works of God. Oh, how we need the power of God in our
churches today!

In the great majority of our churches, much attention is
given to seeing that sinners get saved and come to the
knowledge of Christ. Once they are saved, however, very
little is done to ensure that they receive an anointing of the
Holy Spirit, become effective, and go forth to live victori-
ous lives. Once they are born, we abandon them, in a
sense, and leave them as powerless infants, helpless
against the evil intents of the Enemy.

One reason we don't see the miraculous demonstration of God's power more in our churches these days is because we have religious entertainers in the pulpit. Ministers have been trained to be eloquent orators, and they tell us some very nice things — usually just what we want to hear. After we have listened to several of their soothing sermons, we become complacent and stop seeking God's best for our lives.

Politicians have learned to put a certain "spin" on things so that they become acceptable. Those who work in the news media have done the same. Now, preachers are learning this tactic. It is now possible to sit in their services week after week and never feel uncomfortable, never feel challenged. They make you feel totally satisfied with your present position in God.

This is surely the day of which Amos prophesied:

> *"The days are coming," declares the Sovereign LORD, "when I will send a famine through the land — not a famine of food or a thirst for water, but a famine of hearing the words of the LORD. Men will stagger from sea to sea and wander from north to east, searching for the word of the LORD, but they will not find it. In that day the lovely young women and strong young men will faint because of thirst."*
>
> Amos 8:11-13

Today people travel long distances when they know that the true Word of the Lord is being preached. Because they are so hungry for something more real, challenging, and transforming, it is not uncommon for people to drive sixty miles to church or to go halfway across the country for a special conference. God's Word is being performed. People are hungry for the supernatural.

Believers are infatuated with famous evangelists who have signs and wonders in their ministry. It is not uncommon for Christians to drive clear across the country to see a particular evangelist. The sad thing is that most of those people would never make the sacrifice necessary to see those same miracles in their own lives. A ministry costs something.

People are hungry for the supernatural. Because it cannot be found in their church, many are turning to Eastern religions and "New Age" thinking. Hungry people are susceptible to deceit.

Many devilish practices have been adopted into corporate America in the guise of "productivity training." Outlandish practices are being taught in seminars sponsored by the largest corporations in this country. Many false prophets have entered into the world, and many people are being deceived and are, in turn, deceiving others.

The Church of the Lord Jesus Christ is being called back to basics, to apply itself seriously to battle. We must return to the simple Gospel and to the power of God that enables us to stand against any enemy.

No amount of funding or reeducation can stop this trend toward the occult. The only hope is for God's people to rise up in indignation and take control of the situation. The only hope of reversing the gains of the Enemy is through concerted prayer and fasting.

For more than twenty-four years I have lived for the Word of God. Nothing else is more important to me. It works. I can rely on it. It never fails. I can preach it without reservation. Therefore, I am unwilling to preach the theory of the Word, while never seeing its power in action. I want to see the Word at work. I want to see the power of God transforming lives. I have no interest in playing the church game. I am angry with the devil, and I am determined not to give him one single inch.

I thank God for the miracles I have experienced in my ministry. On four different occasions I have seen the dead raised. (I don't mean people who fainted. I mean people without breath — dead people.) God's power brought them back to life.

Many religious leaders would tell us:

> *That's impossible.*
> *It doesn't happen anymore.*
> *That type of miracle passed away with the apostolic age.*
> *When the disciples died, their gifts died with them.*
> *We cannot expect to see what they saw.*

Yet I have seen cripples walk, just as the original apostles did. I have seen blind eyes opened, just as the apostles did. I have seen the deaf and dumb healed, just as the disciples did. I have watched God heal open sores before my eyes. And it all came because I fasted and prayed, as the apostles did.

One man I prayed for was so mentally ill he had to be chained to a tree. His name was Yeboah, but many referred to him as "the wild animal." Left loose, he recklessly destroyed lives and property. He was so possessed that he ate his own excrement. On several occasions he received supernatural strength and was able to snap the chains that held him. No medicine could seem to sedate him. But I saw him delivered through prayer and fasting. God's power is greater than any other. We can tap that power through prayer and fasting; for prayer and fasting will open your spirit to the supernatural.

Many ministers are preaching more like civil-rights activists these days, instead of like men of deliverance. There is no power in their message; there is no anointing in their hands; and nothing is happening under their leadership. Many of them are good people. They are handsome, intelligent, and caring. But they have lost the power of God. What do they have to offer?

Most of us are impressed by good preaching. "He is a good preacher," we say. "She is a good communicator. She knows how to get her point across." But where are the miracles? Where is the power of God? It is one thing to have a silver tongue and another thing to see and experience the power of God on a regular basis. Preaching can be entertaining without changing our lives at all. It can be pleasant to the ears and be void of power.

Intellect doesn't cast out devils. If it did, we would be calling upon professors to deliver people who are tormented. Men and women of power, whatever their status in life, are used of God to drive away evil spirits.

If your spiritual needs are not being met by your minister, it is time to shake the dust from your feet and go somewhere where you can be fed, somewhere where God's power is in demonstration. I understand that such a move is not always easy. People are reluctant to move from one church to another, for many reasons.

"My grandmother grew up in this church," they say. They have a lot of friends in their old church. And will another church be any better?

---

Prayer and fasting will open your spirit to the supernatural.

---

I understand these reservations, but don't stay in a dead church just because your grandparents were members there. Find a church that means business for God. Your soul and the souls of your other family members are at stake. Look for a church where people love Jesus enough to seek His face and present His Word in power and glory. Look for a church that has more than a few minutes of prayer at a time. Look for a church where fasting is taught and practiced. Any church which has not moved into prayer and fasting is doomed to fail. In every church, those who have serious positions of ministry should be required to fast. Look for a church where this is the case.

I am convinced that most of the miracles, the healings, and the signs and wonders that we see in our ministry are a result of prayer and fasting. Because of that, fasting is not a heavy burden for me. It is a joy. How could I not fast? While some look forward to a good meal, I look forward to the opportunity to shut myself away with God without distraction and draw closer to my heavenly Father.

Any church which has not learned to pray and fast will not have an effective demonstration of the gifts of the Spirit, which are demonstrations of God's power in our midst. Much of what is passing as gifts of the Spirit these days, the prophecies and words of knowledge, are ineffective because many of the people prophesying or giving the word of knowledge have not spent time with God. Their words are shallow. Some who are calling themselves "prophets" have never fasted more than a few hours at a time. They only fast between meals. How could they know the mind of God?

Some people who give a word of knowledge change their minds two or three times before they finally get it out. But God doesn't speak that way. He speaks in specifics. Those people need to do more fasting and praying. God can tell you exactly what's wrong with a person; He can tell you where they live; He can tell you what they like to eat. Let God be specific. Look for a church where genuine gifts, genuine demonstrations of God's power are in evidence.

Many people, when they think of looking for a church home, always think first of "friendliness" or of "love." While it is good to look for loving people, we must remember that the true love of God, His compassion, is only manifested through His power. Everyone has a measure of love, even the people of the world. God's love, His "compassion" is another level of love to which the world can never hope to attain.

The ministry of Jesus was effective because He was *"moved with compassion."*

*But when he saw the multitudes, he was moved with COMPASSION on them, because they fainted, and were scattered abroad, as sheep having no shepherd.*
Matthew 9:36 KJV

*And Jesus went forth, and saw a great multitude, and was moved with COMPASSION toward them, and he healed their sick.*
Matthew 14:14 KJV

*Jesus called his disciples to him and said, "I have COMPASSION for these people; they have already been with me three days and have nothing to eat. I do not want to send them away hungry, or they may collapse on the way."*
Matthew 15:32

*Jesus had COMPASSION on them and touched their eyes. Immediately they received their sight and followed him.*
Matthew 20:34

*Filled with COMPASSION, Jesus reached out his hand and touched the man. "I am willing," he said. "Be clean!"*
Mark 1:41

Jesus was the Son of God, God incarnate. He is love; for God is love. Yet, in order to effectively minister, He had to be moved with compassion. He received this God-breathed love by waiting in the presence of the Father in prayer and fasting.

If Jesus needed a special touch from the Father to effectively minister, how much more we need God to do this great miracle for us! Not all churches that claim to love have genuine compassion. Don't be fooled by substitutes.

An old African proverbs says: *A dead hen cannot hatch fresh eggs*. Put good eggs under a dead hen and the eggs will die too. Something dead cannot give life. Something powerless cannot generate power.

Without prayer and fasting, you cannot see the Gospel's "bottom line." You cannot have God's very best for your life. You cannot experience all that He has promised. The promises of God are not for the carnal. They are not for those who walk in the flesh. They are reserved for those who walk in the Spirit.

Because of its importance, Jesus made fasting a requirement for the church. He said:

> *"How can the guests of the bridegroom mourn while he is with them? The time will come when the bridegroom will be taken from them; then they will fast."*
> Matthew 9:15

Considering their lack of prayer and fasting, it is no wonder that most churches rarely see a miracle. It is no wonder that the power of God is never manifested in their midst. **God's power comes to those who seek Him.**

# Chapter 11

## *The Need for More Faith*

*Therefore, since the promise of entering his rest still stands, let us be careful that none of you be found to have fallen short of it. For we also have had the gospel preached to us, just as they did; but the message they heard was of no value to them, because those who heard did not combine it with faith. Now we who have believed enter that rest, just as God has said, "So I declared on oath in my anger, 'They shall never enter my rest.' " And yet his work has been finished since the creation of the world.*     Hebrews 4:1-3

The promises of God have been given to people down through the centuries. When these promises were not believed, however, when the Word was not *"combined with faith*," there was no result. God's blessings are not automatic. The Word *"combined with faith"* produces God's blessings in our lives.

Those who believe the Word of God enter into God's *"rest."* That means that if you receive the Word of God and walk by faith, you always have rest in the Lord. Nothing disturbs your peace. Nothing perturbs you. Those who do not obey this admonition live in constant turmoil and confusion.

Nothing could be more important in our Christian lives than our faith. We are saved by faith. We are healed by faith. We receive miracles by faith. We receive and operated the gifts of the Spirit by faith. Everything we do is by faith. And, as we have already seen:

> *And without faith it is impossible to please God, because anyone who comes to him must believe that he exists and that he rewards those who earnestly seek him.*                    Hebrews 11:6

God is pleased when we believe Him. He loves us and wants the very best for us. Everything that He does is for our benefit. Our faith in His goodness sets in motion the forces of the universe. Our faith, then, is founded on HIM.

> *For we do not have a high priest who is unable to sympathize with our weaknesses, but we have one who has been tempted in every way, just as we are — yet was without sin. Let us then approach the throne of grace with confidence, so that we may receive mercy and find grace to help us in our time of need.*
> Hebrews 4:15-16

Jesus is our High Priest. He was able to take His own shed blood into the presence of God. With His blood He made a covenant with us. Now, we are covered with His blood. Because of that, we can come *"with confidence"* into His presence. This is the basis of our faith.

Our faith is not based on what we see. Airplanes leave a trail of smoke in the sky. Sometimes we can see the smoke and not the airplane. We may not be able to see the Lord with our physical eyes, but He is always there. What a wonderful High Priest we have!

We need to wake up with faith for a wonderful day. We need to walk in faith that God is watching out for us and that everything will be done for our good. We need to go to church with faith that we are going to meet God and that He is going to touch us in the area of our need.

Many people go to church with serious problems. They listen to the preaching or the teaching, but are unable to take advantage of what they are hearing. They cannot appropriate it. The message goes in one ear and out the other.

The problem is not that Jesus doesn't understand the situation. He does. He was tempted in every way. He knows what drug addicts go through. He understands the economic pressures that force some women (and some men) into prostitution. He is able to deal with any and every situation. There is no conceivable problem that is too great for Him. The problem is that we need to believe Him. We need to get our mind on Him and talk to Him — in faith.

When Peter was about to sink in the waters of the Sea of Galilee, he prayed a prayer of desperation for God to save him. He could pray that prayer because he had taken a leap of faith and started walking on the water to Jesus. Most people who pray desperate prayers have so little faith that He can't even hear them.

Paul wrote to the Romans:

> *For therein is the righteousness of God revealed from faith to faith: as it is written, The just shall live by faith.* Romans 1:17 KJV

*"The just shall live by faith."* Faith isn't just some mental assent. It is a way of life. It affects everything that we do. It makes us walk right and talk right. *"The just shall live by faith."* Their faith will produce the proper works. Because they believe they will act on that belief.

> *In the same way, faith by itself, if it is not accompanied by action, is dead.* James 2:17

A person who doesn't put their faith to work is like a brother who has lost his job. He may have many abilities, but he will soon go bankrupt, because he is not working.

A corporation may have a name and a legal status, but if it produces nothing and accomplishes nothing, it will soon falter.

Faith that doesn't produce is meaningless. It is dead. Most Christians have faith, but their faith is no longer breathing or their faith is a negative faith.

Faith works in two directions. There is a positive faith and there is a negative faith. They are equally powerful.

Many Christians expect all the worst things to happen to them, and they do.

Let your faith be both positive and living. Let it produce the appropriate action. If you aren't willing to get up in the morning and put forth an effort to support your family, you soon won't have a family to support. You can wake up every morning and quote dozens of Scriptures, but if you do nothing, your faith is vain. It accomplishes nothing.

Action pleases God. It proves your faith. Faith pleases God and displeases Satan. He knows whether we believe or not. He knows whether we depend on God or not. He knows if we spend time with the heavenly Father or not. He knows if we wait in the presence of God for power and authority over him or not.

And here we have the relationship between more faith and prayer and fasting. If we spend time with the Father, our faith grows. The better we know Him and the more we know about His power and glory, the more our faith grows. Because we know more about the Lord, we have more faith in Him and in His Word.

Satan trembles when we pray and fast. He knows that we are receiving faith to cast down his kingdom. He hates fasting. He will do anything to keep us from obeying God in prayer and fasting. **ANYTHING!**

Satan knows that if we don't mix the Word with faith, nothing will happen. He knows that if we don't pray with faith, our prayers will not be answered.

> *"IF YOU BELIEVE, you will receive whatever you ask for in prayer."* Matthew 21:22

*" 'If you can'?" said Jesus. "Everything is possible*
*FOR HIM WHO BELIEVES."*                      Mark 9:23

*"I tell you the truth, if anyone says to this mountain,*
*'Go, throw yourself into the sea,' and does not doubt*
*in his heart but BELIEVES that what he says will*
*happen, it will be done for him. Therefore I tell you,*
*whatever you ask for in prayer, BELIEVE that you*
*have received it, and it will be yours.*
                                              Mark 11:23-24

Satan knows that if we don't believe, we will not be
healed and delivered from his afflictions.

*Then Jesus said to the centurion, "Go! It will be done*
*JUST AS YOU BELIEVED it would." And his ser-*
*vant was healed at that very hour.*
                                              Matthew 8:13

Jesus taught us to pray always, to pray in the will of God
for our lives (not to pray *"amiss"*), and to pray with faith.
Even then, many prayers will not be answered without
fasting.

Hannah desperately wanted a son and believed that it
was God's will to give her a son. She promised God that if
He would bless her with such a child, she would dedicate
him to serve the Lord. Hannah fasted and prayed and
believed God for the miracle. And God responded to her
exercise of faith.

When Peter was cast into prison, he was constantly
guarded by four soldiers. His enemies intended to kill

him just as soon as Passover had ended. He was causing too much trouble preaching about Jesus Christ and His miracles.

---

If we spend time with the Father, our faith grows. The better we know Him and the more we know about His power and glory, the more our faith grows. Because we know more about the Lord, we have more faith in Him and in His Word.

---

But, before they could do that, something unusual happened. The angel of the Lord visited that prison. He woke Peter up and told him to get his sandals on. Then he led him out past the guards. The gate opened of its own accord, and Peter was set free. It all happened because believers were praying in the home of Mary, the mother of John Mark.

It was late at night, and no doubt many of them were sleepy. They could have been home in bed getting a good night's rest, but they had dedicated themselves to intercede for Peter.

While they were praying, someone knocked at the door. It was Peter. He didn't rush out to celebrate his freedom at the all-night corner restaurant. Some people lose three pounds fasting and put on six the next day by gorging at their celebration banquet.

When he was released from prison, Peter went straight to the house where he knew believers would be gathered praying. Sure enough, when he arrived, he heard them still praying. He knocked on the door. The door was opened by a slave girl named Rhoda. She recognized him. Becoming very excited, she went back inside to tell the others the good news. But they couldn't believe it and wondered if she were having hallucinations. Only when the door was opened did they see that God had indeed heard their cry.

When we pray, are we expecting God to answer? Are we expecting something to happen? Are we looking for the miracle that God will do?

**Prayer and fasting sharpens your expectancy so that when you ask, you expect to receive.**

# Chapter 12

## *The Need for Preparation*

*"Therefore everyone who hears these words of mine and puts them into practice is like a wise man who built his house on the rock. The rain came down, the streams rose, and the winds blew and beat against that house; yet it did not fall, because it had its foundation on the rock. But everyone who hears these words of mine and does not put them into practice is like a foolish man who built his house on sand. The rain came down, the streams rose, and the winds blew and beat against that house, and it fell with a great crash."*
Matthew 7:24-27

*"He is like a man building a house, who dug down deep and laid the foundation on rock. When a flood came, the torrent struck that house but could not*

*shake it, because it was well built. But the one who
hears my words and does not put them into practice is
like a man who built a house on the ground without a
foundation. The moment the torrent struck that
house, it collapsed and its destruction was complete."*

Luke 6:48-49

A wise man builds on the rock. His house is powerful. It
will withstand every storm. A foolish man builds on the
sand. His house is not well supported. When storms
come, as they must, it will fall. In this parable, Jesus was
instructing us about the need for a proper foundation, the
need for proper preparation for life.

Some people ask, "Why doesn't God hear our prayers?"
Lack of faith may be one important element of the answer,
but only one element. Lack of preparation has to be another important element. Nothing could be more
important!

A student cannot depend on faith when exam day ar-
rives. He or she must prepare. When a person is
unprepared, it shows up — regardless of how much faith
they might have.

*To prepare* means *the process of making something ready
before hand for use. Preparation* means *getting something ready
for a project.*

In recent years we have come to recognize the need for
preparation in many aspects of life. During that same period we have come to neglect the most important elements
of spiritual preparation.

In the business world, successful people are prepared
people. Some poorly prepared people seem to obtain a

level of success, but it is rarely lasting. Credentials mean everything in the work place today. As we move further into the technical era, they become increasingly important.

It is more difficult to document spiritual preparation, but it is no less important.

Preparation is crucial in the military, and there are no shortcuts. Soldiers who are not well prepared do not last long in time of war. With the first enemy attacks they are easily defeated.

---

"Why doesn't God hear our prayers?" Lack of faith may be one important element of the answer, but only one element. Lack of preparation has to be another important element. Nothing could be more important!

---

The training to which modern athletes submit themselves should challenge us all. They train many hours a day. Some professional football players lift weights for four hours every day, just to toughen themselves up. They not only train physically, they train themselves mentally and emotionally, as well.

Athletes are motivated by the joy of winning. They are motivated by the fame their position brings them. And they are motivated by the money they can make in professional sports. We have much more to gain, or much more to lose — depending on your perspective.

We all recognize the importance of preparation in some areas of life:

Would you like to go to a doctor who was not well prepared?

Would you like to cross a long bridge designed by an engineer who was not well-prepared?

But how many recognize that, because our society has become so complicated, it is now impossible to be a good husband or wife without preparation? How many know that it is impossible to be a good father or mother without being prepared?

Many of the men in the African-American segment of our society are being destroyed. Many are in prison. Many are involved in illegal activities. The reason so many are failing is that they don't have a set goal in life to work toward, and they don't see the importance of preparation.

Because our men are failing, women have to take all the responsibility for the family. When they have to work outside the home, often the children are neglected. Children are not taking their studies seriously enough. Many of them lack initiative — because their parents are not well-prepared for life and are thus poor examples to them.

*Preparation* is not a pleasant word to most of us. It speaks of time and effort, both of which we don't want to "waste." It is true that preparation takes time. It is true that preparation takes effort. But everything in life that is worthwhile takes time and effort and is worth the time and effort we put into it.

We don't like the sound of the word *preparation* because we have become a society that looks for shortcuts. We cook by microwave. We travel by high-speed jets. We communicate by modems and faxes. We want to learn everything in a few easy steps or from a "HOW TO" manual. Nobody wants to do homework anymore. Nobody wants to put in the time necessary to excel.

Christians are no different. We want to receive Bible results, but we don't want to pay the Bible price. We are always looking for shortcuts. We want to be blessed, but we don't want to do what is necessary to get that blessing. So we serve God when we feel like it. We serve God when it is convenient. We serve God when it seems to fit into our over-all scheme of life. Or we serve God when we need Him. Otherwise, we don't have either the time or the energy to dedicate to His purpose.

When you are unprepared, your life is in danger. You are subject to constant attack by the Enemy of your soul. He sees you as an easy target. Time spent in preparation is not time wasted. Preparation enables you to accomplish your purpose in life. If you are not prepared, you will fail.

It took me nearly twenty-four years to understand why I had power and authority over the works of the Enemy. There is no devil (no demon) in Africa, in India, in South America, in the United States, or in Europe that can defeat me if I maintain my relationship to God through prayer and fasting. All of them put together cannot defeat me. They can attack me, but they cannot win. You can tell them I said so. They know where I live. That's how powerful a force prayer and fasting is in my life! I have that assurance just as certainly as I have the assurance of salvation.

I know, beyond any shadow of a doubt, that I am saved. No one can convince me otherwise. I am confident in the Word of God. Nobody can tell me that it is not true. And, in the same way, and to the same degree, nothing can change my mind as to my authority and power over the works of the Enemy. As a prepared Christian, I know where I stand, and I can boldly state my case.

Ministers of the Gospel need to be well-prepared. Many don't want to make the effort or spend the time to prepare themselves fully. When God gives them a ministerial gift they think that means that they have nothing at all to do. That isn't the case. They need to prepare for the ministry to which God has called them. Some try to launch out into their ministry before they are ready, and they fail because they put the proverbial cart before the horse. Take time to sit and be trained. Don't get impatient.

One minister, whom I recognize as an outstanding teacher, has been affiliated with my ministry for many years. At the time of this writing, he is still being trained. He recognizes that and doesn't leap ahead of God but fully submits to me as his pastor.

Another minister I know quite well is so full of God that I love to hear him preach. If you have any discouragement at all, get close to him and your discouragement will vanish. He is that kind of man. Yet, for a period of time, he went with me everywhere I went and carried my Bible. He was in training.

There are many other promising ministers that I know who are very capable people and have great futures, but they are content for now to prepare themselves fully. Not everyone is that wise.

Some people can't sit anytime at all. They want to go out and change the world NOW. That's fine; but you can't do it if you are not prepared. The Lone Ranger apparently made a popular TV hero for children, but God doesn't honor any Lone Rangers today. He wants a prepared people. Whatever your particular gift is, whatever your vocation in life, let God prepare you for the days ahead.

As a pastor and professor, I cannot stand in front of my congregation or my college class and expect to feed my people if I have not prepared myself. How can I give something I do not have? What would you think if your mother called you to the dinner table, but forgot to prepare anything for the meal? It's a crazy thought, isn't it! Believe me, it is just as crazy to try to do God's work without the proper preparation.

Some people seem to get by with little preparation until they experience a crisis. When they are attacked by the Enemy, they don't know how to react properly. What they do sometimes isn't very "Christian."

Some people can only take a defensive stance at everything because they have never been trained at offense. In sports, defense is important, but those teams which ultimately take the top prizes also excel at offense. They are extremely well-prepared.

When God called me to preach the Gospel, I knew I had to prepare. I remember telling my mother what God had laid on my heart. She had wanted me to become an engineer.

I spent most of my vacation time that year preaching, and I loved it; but I decided not to drop out of college. I could finish and not do it for the flesh but for the Lord.

I knew my purpose in life. I knew my destiny. I knew that I had a message for my generation, but I was determined to give God my best. I refused to quit, although that decision would have been very acceptable to most of my peers.

If any man on the continent of Africa wanted to serve God, it was me. If any man was willing to believe His Word, it was me. If any man was anxious to preach, it was me. But I was also willing to pay any price to prepare for the Lord's work.

The day I graduated, I packed my bag and started a little church in someone's single-stall garage in a little village. I lived right there. I put a blanket over two wooden benches, and that was my bed. I stayed there for a year. I wasn't afraid to take chances for God. My heart was prepared. My mind was prepared. And I was willing to pay the price.

Prayer and fasting is an important element in any spiritual preparation, whether it be for life or for ministry. Jesus was well-prepared to live as an example of the Christian life, and He was well-prepared for the ministry entrusted to Him by His Father. Because He had waited in the presence of the Father, He could boldly say:

> *"The Spirit of the Lord is on me, because he has anointed me to preach good news to the poor. He has sent me to proclaim freedom for the prisoners and recovery of sight for the blind, to release the oppressed, to proclaim the year of the Lord's favor."*
>
> Luke 4:18-19

I thank God for the privilege of prayer and fasting. After more than twenty-four years I am still preparing myself. I haven't arrived. Every day holds new challenges for me and the greatest days are just ahead.

And life itself is a preparation for something greater. One day soon we will present ourselves at the Marriage Supper of the Lamb. **I want to be prepared for that day, as well.**

# Chapter 13

## *The Need for a Healthy Life-style*

*Then shall thy light break forth as the morning, and THINE HEALTH SHALL SPRING FORTH SPEEDILY: and thy righteousness shall go before thee; the glory of the Lord shall be thy rereward.*

Isaiah 58:8 KJV

Although losing weight is not our primary purpose in fasting, fasting is a very healthy custom to adopt. While we bring the flesh into subjection to the Spirit of God and develop a deeper relationship with our heavenly Father, we get the side benefit of a more healthy body. There are several reasons for this:

When you fast, your system has time to heal itself. It gives your internal organs time to rest and recuperate. They work very hard most of the time. No wonder they occasionally rebel! Most of us abuse our digestive systems with the wrong kinds of food over a long period. More and more doctors are realizing how healthy it is to let the system have a time of restoration.

---

Although losing weight is not our primary purpose in fasting, fasting is a very healthy custom to adopt.

---

When we fast our system is cleansed. In measure, this happens while we sleep. But we don't always wake up in the morning ready to conquer the world. Sometimes more time is needed to flush all the toxins out of our systems.

Uncontrolled eating does all sorts of damage to the body. Periods of fasting bring the body into balance and help to regulate the systems so that things run more smoothly.

Although God's people don't have the harmful habits of drinking, smoking and doing drugs, so many of them are killing themselves with food — too much food and the wrong kinds of food. This cannot be pleasing to God.

Many fear that fasting is harmful to your health. Moses fasted forty days; but he did not have to be carried down from the mountain. And when he came down, his face glowed with the glory of the Lord.

If you follow God's leading in fasting, you will not grow unduly weak. You will not ruin your health. Ladies, fasting will not destroy the beauty of your skin. If you fast enough, the glory of the Lord will shine forth from you, as it did from the face of Moses. Believe the promise of God: *"THINE HEALTH SHALL SPRING FORTH SPEEDILY."*

This will be accomplished through the resting of your organs, through the cleansing of your system, through getting control of your appetites and developing a more health-conscious life-style and through the miraculous touch of God upon your life. **Fasting is a very healthy custom to adopt.**

# Part IV

# How You Can
# Pray and Fast
# More Effectively
# (Preparation)

# Chapter 14

## *Make a Commitment to PRAYER AND FASTING*

*Behold, I will pour out my spirit unto you, I will make known my words unto you.* Proverbs 1:23 KJV

The first step to successful prayer and fasting is to make a commitment to do it. That commitment is finalized by making a proclamation, by making known your intentions.

The word *preach* comes from the same Greek word *caruso*. It means *to proclaim, to make known or declare*. When Jesus spoke to those people in the synagogue of Nazareth, He said that the Spirit of the Lord was upon Him to proclaim, to make known, and to declare the Gospel to the poor. The Spirit of the Lord was upon Him to heal the brokenhearted. The Spirit of the Lord was upon Him to proclaim, to make known and to declare deliverance to the captives. And the Spirit of the Lord was upon Him to proclaim, to make known, and to declare the acceptable year of the Lord.

Proclamation, or making something known, is very important. The Scriptures declare:

> *For it is with your heart that you believe and are justified, and it is with your mouth that you confess and are saved.*                    Romans 10:10

We confess the Lord Jesus Christ and we are saved. In this sense, every Christian is called to be a preacher, one who proclaims. The first person we must preach to is ourself. We must speak God's Word to ourselves. If not, we can never speak God's Word to others.

Once is not enough. Every day we need to remind ourselves of the grace of God in our lives. We need to proclaim, to make known and declare God's favor toward us frequently.

When I have declared my faith to others, they are justified in expecting me to live up to my confession or "profession" of faith. When they look at me, they may do so based on the declaration I have made. I am bound by my confession. When I tell someone that I am saved, they expect to see new life in me. When I say that I love the Lord, people are justified in expecting to see that declaration lived out in my words and my actions.

When we make a declaration, we are not just speaking empty words. We must believe what we declare. Toward the end of every year, people begin making their New Year's resolutions. Some resolve to lose weight. Others resolve to stop smoking or to break some other bad habit. The great majority keep these well-meaning resolutions for only a few days. They didn't believe what they were resolving in the first place. They weren't serious and didn't make a commitment from the heart. Caught up in the emotion of the passing of another year, they resolved. But their resolve wasn't very effective. Our proclamation, our commitment must be different than human resolve.

---

The first step to successful prayer and fasting is to make a commitment to do it. That commitment is finalized by making a proclamation, by making known your intentions.

---

Most Christians have, at one time or another, made a commitment to fast "after Thanksgiving." But after Thanksgiving, someone invites us to KFC and offers us some of those large biscuits. Then Christmas comes, and New Years, and birthdays, and the 4th of July, and on, and on, and on. It never ends. There are enough special days in the year to keep us breaking our resolve forever.

With many people, because there is not a firm commitment to fasting, any excuse will do to avoid it. It doesn't take much. This is why it is necessary to make a proclamation concerning fasting. You must personally make a statement, to yourself and others, that you intend to fast for a certain period of time. Once made, you must keep your commitment; for making a confession places you in a position of responsibility before God and before man.

Many people are fearful of commitment. They know it costs something. They are afraid that they may not be able to fulfill their part of the commitment. They say they would rather not promise and have to break that promise. This is a phony excuse. When you use that excuse, you are making a commitment to failure and to mediocrity.

When I invite people to come to church, some answer: "Pastor, I don't want to promise you that I will come, because something might happen that I couldn't make it. Please don't count on me. I will try to make it — if I can."

I doubt if that type of person will ever fully understand the Kingdom of God. They would have to say: "Well Lord, I want to come. But don't count on me. I might not make it." How can you place authority or trust in people who are afraid to make any commitment? You can't!

James said:

*He is a double-minded man, unstable in all he does.*
                                              James 1:8

Make up your mind. If you want to be part of God's Kingdom, then make a commitment to do it. If you want to receive the blessings of a local church, then make a commitment to be an active part of that church. If you want to hear God's voice, make a commitment to pray and fast.

Just prior to verse 8, James said:

*But when he asks, he must believe and not doubt,*
*because he who doubts is like a wave of the sea, blown*
*and tossed by the wind. That man should not think he*
*will receive anything from the Lord;*    James 1:6-7

That is strong language. *"That man should not think that*
*he will receive anything from the Lord."* **ANYTHING!** God
cannot trust such a person. They are not reliable. Their line
is always: "Well, I am not going to tell you that I will do
this. I would like to, but perhaps I can't. And I wouldn't
want to disappoint you." What a lame excuse! And so
many people use it.

It is better to commit and have to break a commitment
and suffer the consequences than never to make a commitment of any kind. Those who never make a commitment
to fast never fast.

This half hearted approach to everything seems to be
acceptable in our society today: No commitment in marriage, no commitment on the job, no commitment in the
church, no commitment among friends. If you commit
yourself, you might have to do something whether you
want to or not. So, why take the chance?

When we ask someone to do something in the church,
instead of jumping at the chance to honor the Lord by
their involvement, they say, "I'm not sure. Give me time to
pray about it. That's a big commitment."

No wonder few people fast! It demands too much
of them!

I understand why many Christians have so little joy.
They are not willing to make a full commitment to Christ.

They are trying to live on the fence, with one foot in the Kingdom and the other in the flesh. And it simply won't work. People who live like that are the most miserable people alive. They are more miserable than sinners. At least sinners know where they stand.

To reap the benefits of prayer and fasting, you must make a commitment and stick with your commitment. You must make a commitment of time and effort to dedicate to prayer and fasting. If something legitimate prevents you from doing it, make a new commitment and keep it this time.

You cannot expect results from your faith if you are unwilling to make a full commitment to Him Who is the object of your faith. You cannot expect to see the Word of God fulfilled in your life if you are unwilling to make a full commitment to the Word. It's worth it. Believe me.

I have faith in the Word of God. I am not afraid to make a full commitment to live by His Word. I know the power of God that comes through prayer and fasting, and I am not afraid to make a commitment to pray and fast. It's worth it.

Do you have difficulty committing yourself to eat? Is that a chore for you? Do you keep postponing your meals because you have so many other more important things to do? I don't think so. You eat because it is important to you. You know the benefits. If we could understand all the good that fasting will do for us, we would be anxious to fast, delighted to fast, and looking for an opportunity to do so.

Is it a struggle for you to go to the dinner table? Then why is it such a struggle for you not to go to the dinner table? Is your god your belly? Does flesh rule your life? Make a commitment and keep it.

When you proclaim a fast, the devil will tell you that you are a hypocrite, trying to draw attention to yourself. The Bible does say:

> But when you give to the needy, do not let your left hand know what your right hand is doing,
>
> Matthew 6:3

That means that we are not to boast about what we are doing. It is to be done "unto God." That, however, does not prevent us from declaring what we are about to do.

Some people really put on a show when they fast. They try to look absolutely miserable. They don't bathe. They keep looking in the mirror to see how their condition is — as if they were about to die at any minute. "Do I look pale to you?" they ask. "Are my lips white?"

The declaration I am talking about is not for vainglory. It is to get yourself and others around you ready for what you are about to do. It is making a commitment so that you will not be able to easily change your mind for every flimsy excuse. I find that declaring my fast eliminates much of the struggle I might otherwise have in obeying God.

In order to make a declaration to fast, you must first be convinced that you should do it. Uncertainty always leads to procrastination. There are many ways that this can be accomplished.

It is very biblical for a pastor or other leader to call for the entire congregation to fast. Some people rebel and say,

"I fast when the Lord tells me to fast. I don't fast just because the pastor says I should. God can speak to me personally." Those people almost never fast. If they are unwilling to join a public fast, they rarely fast on their own.

If a fast is not called by a spiritual leader, it becomes a very personal thing — between you and God. Give Him opportunity to speak to you. God doesn't tell some people to fast because they don't want to hear it. Their ears are stopped. Their mind is made up. God doesn't tell them to fast because He doesn't waste words. If you are open, He will speak to you.

If many months go by, and you haven't been led to fast, get concerned. That is not normal. The disciples fasted regularly. So did many of the congregations of the Great Reformation. Read God's Word until you become convinced of your need to fast. Then make your commitment.

You will be very hesitant to make a commitment to prayer and fasting if you doubt your ability to fulfill such a commitment. Those who are unsure can start out with shorter periods of fasting. There is no biblical rule about how long you must fast. Begin on a smaller scale and work your way up as you feel able.

Perhaps you have been feeling a little weak physically and are not sure if you can complete a fast. Perhaps you are not feeling the best because of a recent bout of flu or because of extra hours put into work or some physical strain. There is no better way to improve your health and receive divine healing than fasting.

If you are unsure of the timing of your fast — when you should begin and how long you should fast — you may hesitate to make a commitment. It isn't always necessary to know how long you will go before you begin. If the Lord leads you to begin and doesn't tell you how long to fast, trust Him to tell you when it is time to quit. Make a commitment to fast until the Lord tells you to stop fasting.

If you feel burdened to fast and don't know when to begin, know that **the same God who urges you to fast can tell you exactly when to do it**.

# Chapter 15

## *Prepare Yourself*
## *for*
## *PRAYER AND FASTING*

*But I keep under my body, and bring it into subjec-*
*tion: lest that by any means, when I have preached to*
*others, I myself should be a castaway.*
                                        1 Corinthians 9:27  KJV

Your declaration, your commitment to prayer and fasting is more for yourself than it is for others. When I declare
that I am going to fast, I am taking the first step toward
preparing myself. I am putting every part of my being on
alert, letting every part of my body know what I intend to
do. My mind is made up. My emotions are under control.
I know exactly what I am about to do. I will fast and seek
the face of God.

Once I have made that declaration, the responsibility to carry though on my commitment is mine, and I must prepare myself to obey. I must discipline myself and make myself fast. Those who really love God and mean business with Him do that. No one said it would be easy. Make yourself fast. Give yourself a challenge. Say to yourself:

*I will bring my spirit, my body, my emotions and my mind all under subjection to the Word of God by giving myself to prayer and fasting.*

Get yourself ready to do something great. God does not waste a prepared vessel. He has much work to be done and is looking for those who are ready to be placed into positions of authority.

It is amazing to meet some worldly business people and see their positive attitude toward life. They expect the best to happen. They never expect the worst. They are optimistic about the economy and their future in it and are preparing themselves to do well.

It is amazing to speak with career military people. They believe that one day they will be great officers. They are very positive and upbeat. They are working very hard and making great sacrifices toward their goal.

It is amazing to meet serious athletes. They believe they can be the best and are putting extraordinary effort into achieving their long-term goals. They are excited about what they are doing.

Then it is amazing to meet Christians who have all the promises of the Word of God. The future is clearly laid out for them in Scripture many times and they have been told often that they are on the winning team. Yet they are so negative about everything and so lax about taking the steps necessary to bring about God's will in their lives.

This is a tragedy because we have the answer for the drug addicts of our city. They don't need a secular rehabilitation program. We can help them. We know the God of love. He will deliver them. We can help their families. We can help their loved ones.

---

When I declare that I am going to fast, I am taking the first step toward preparing myself. I am putting every part of my being on alert, letting every part of my body know what I intend to do. My mind is made up. My emotions are under control. I know exactly what I am about to do.

---

We have the answer for the homeless and the downtrodden. We should be the most motivated people in the world.

We have the answer for unwed mothers. They don't need to look elsewhere. We know how to take wayward girls off the street. In our fellowship, they can find hope and comfort.

We have the answer to people trapped on welfare. We can help them. We can train them. We can equip them.

We have the answer for the hungry, the lost, the cold, the oppressed. We have the answer for precious children with chemical imbalances, whose parents are desperate to find what is wrong with their children. God's love can rescue them and make them normal and healthy.

With the power that comes with regular prayer and fasting, we will see our lost loved ones come into the fold. We will see suffering grandmothers and mothers (who have been given up by medical science, and who are preparing their wills because they don't expect to live long), totally healed and delivered.

A Christianity that doesn't reach out beyond the four walls of the church stinks. It is not Christianity at all. God sent His Son to die for our sins because He loved the whole world.

> *"For God so loved the world that he gave his one and only Son, that whoever believes in him shall not perish but have eternal life."*                    John 3:16

We can have His love and take it to the world — if we are willing to pay the price of prayer and fasting. Get yourself prepared for all that God has for you. Set your sights on the goal. Look toward the goal, *"to win the prize."*

> *I press on toward the goal to win the prize for which God has called me heavenward in Christ Jesus.*
> Philippians 3:14

Instruct your spirit man. Let it be known in every part of your body that you intend to seek God and do His will.

Equip yourself with the Word of the Lord. Let fasting become your desire. Make a point of giving yourself to fasting. There is no other way.

Say without fear:

> *Belly, I want you to know that Christ is in control of my life. You no longer have authority. You will obey — whether you like it or not.*
>
> *Belly, I want you to understand that because God is in charge of my life, God is in charge of YOU. You cannot rule me any longer. I have given my life completely to the Lord, and I intend to do His will.*

If you are having a struggle in this area, repeat out loud this declaration:

> *I am determined to bring my flesh under subjection to the Spirit of God because I want God's best for my life. I refuse to walk in the flesh any longer. From this day forward I will walk in the Spirit so that I will not fulfill the desires of the flesh. I will allow God to glorify His name through my life. I will obey Him in prayer and fasting.*

Put the flesh on notice, without delay.

The next step in your preparation seems, on the surface, to be a purely physical one: Begin to adjust your body to the new reality. Some people eat many times a day. When they decide to fast, their body is shocked. They may experience symptoms very similar to drug withdrawal. They may get dizzy; they may feel weak; and their stomach may ache. These people need special preparation. Leading up to their fast, they should start reducing the number of times they eat each day so that fasting will not be such a terrible shock to their system.

If you eat three regular meals a day, cut back to two, then to one. Then your body won't be shocked when you deny it food altogether for your period of prayer and fasting.

If you drink coffee regularly, begin to cut back, so that you won't get headaches when you fast.

Those who are especially susceptible to the temptation to overindulge their appetites must be careful to inform their senses what to expect in the days ahead. They must put their flesh on notice. The shock some people experience is as much psychological and emotional as it is physical.

This is serious business which demands sincerity and dedication. Don't be lax in your preparation — either physically, emotionally, psychologically or spiritually.

**Get ready for the great things God has for you.**

# Chapter 16

## *Stop Making Excuses! JUST DO IT!*

*"But they all alike began to make excuses."*
                                            Luke 14:18

Just like those who were invited to the wedding feast, everyone seems to have their own excuse for not fasting.

### Young People and FASTING

Some young people think they are "too young" to fast. When our daughter, Anna, was very young we allowed her to miss a meal occasionally, even though she was too young to understand well what she was doing. She couldn't know about the needs of the local church. She couldn't know about the problems of the ministry.

Nevertheless, by permitting her to fast, we knew that we were equipping her early to know how to seek the face of God.

If all of us had begun to pray and fast at a younger age, many of us would not have gotten into so many problems in adolescence and young adulthood. I thank God for parents who encouraged me in prayer and fasting. They wanted more than anything else to see me in the will of God for my life.

---

If all of us had begun to pray and fast at a younger age, many of us would not have gotten into so many problems in adolescence and young adulthood.

---

Young people, don't let anyone tell you that fasting is not of God or is no longer important. Don't let anyone tell you that YOU don't need to fast. Don't let your belly run your life. Take authority over your appetites. Get your life under control. Submit yourself to God so that you can get your every prayer answered.

Remember, when the disciples asked, *"Why couldn't we do it? What is the secret?"*, Jesus answered them, *"This kind goes not out but by prayer and fasting."* Stand on the word of Jesus and don't let anyone discourage you from doing His will for your life. As young people, you have a whole lifetime ahead of you. Don't waste your opportunities. Get serious with God and His blessing will be upon you.

Parents, don't deny your children and young people the opportunity to seek the face of God in prayer and fasting, if and when they desire to do it.

## The Elderly and FASTING

Some elderly people think they are "too old" to fast. If you are a diabetic, perhaps you have a legitimate reason not to fast — until you get set free from your sickness. I have known many people who received healing from various diseases while they were fasting. Don't limit God.

For those elderly persons who are well, there is no excuse. Anna the prophetess should be an example to every elderly person concerning fasting.

> *There was also a prophetess, Anna, the daughter of Phanuel, of the tribe of Asher. She was very old; she had lived with her husband seven years after her marriage, and then was a widow until she was eighty-four. She never left the temple but worshiped night and day, fasting and praying. Coming up to them at that very moment, she gave thanks to God and spoke about the child to all who were looking forward to the redemption of Jerusalem.*
>
> Luke 2:36-38

Anna fasted regularly, although she was *"very old."* Fasting and prayer developed in her a sensitivity to the Spirit of God so that when most everyone failed to recognize the child Jesus as being any different from other children of a similar age, Anna was miraculously drawn to Him.

Elderly people don't want to fast for the same reason the rest of us don't want to fast. We have accustomed our stomachs to certain foods at certain times of the day, and we don't like to feel hungry. We enjoy eating.

---

Elderly people don't want to fast for the same reason the rest of us don't want to fast.

---

The elderly are among those who have no tolerance for church services that go a few minutes beyond mealtime. When the internal alarm clock goes off, they forget what God is saying and concentrate on getting out of the church so they can eat. At that point, many close their hearts and minds to anything else. Nothing is more important to them than eating.

I would say to the elderly among us that God hasn't finished with you yet. You have a very great responsibility before God to share your knowledge of Him with the upcoming generations. Be the examples you should be in prayer and fasting.

## Men and FASTING

Some men don't fast because they believe they must constantly spend time with their family. If you, as the leader of your household, cannot hear the voice of God and know God's will for your family, you are not a good father anyway.

Some men never fast because they have to work and they cannot get alone with God for long periods. If you must work, that doesn't mean that you cannot fast. Many of God's people who have to work fast anyway. Just ask the Lord to help you keep your mind on Him. When lunch time comes, don't hang around to see what the others will eat. Get alone, perhaps in your car or in some other private place. Get your Bible and concentrate on the mind of the Lord. But fast.

---

If you must work, that doesn't mean that you cannot fast.

---

Men, we have a great responsibility. Because we know that we are living in the last days and that the coming of the Lord is growing nearer, we should be compelled to pray and fast more. Those who are not conscious of the lateness of the hour never fast.

*Jesus answered, "How can the guests of the bride-groom fast while he is with them? They cannot, so long as they have him with them. But the time will come when the bridegroom will be taken from them, and on that day THEY WILL FAST."*

Mark 2:19-20

Jesus said that we should fast when the bridegroom was taken away. Fasting will continue, then, until His return. Don't stop now. There is too much to be accomplished in the Kingdom of God.

After twenty-four years in the ministry, God is dealing with me to fast more than ever. This is not a time to relax and allow ourselves to be ruled by the flesh. We must hone our spiritual instincts and be ready to do spiritual warfare in these last days. Don't let the women do all the fasting. If we do, they get all the blessings.

## Women and FASTING

In general, women fast more than men. But even many women have their excuses not to do it. The two most predominant excuses women use are their need to prepare food for the whole family and their need to maintain a good appearance. Neither of these need be an excuse not to fast when the Lord leads you to do so.

> If you need to prepare food for the rest of the family, you can do that and continue your fast. It just demands a little more willpower on your part not to eat everything you are cooking.

If you need to prepare food for the rest of the family, you can do that and continue your fast. It just demands a little more willpower on your part not to eat everything you are cooking. While your husband and your children eat, read your Bible. Meditate on the goodness of God. You can serve others, while abstaining yourself.

As for appearance, it is a lie of Satan that fasting destroys your appearance. My mother is nearly seventy now. Yet, she is strong and looks fresh and beautiful — because of her life of fasting and prayer.

Women, stop believing Satan's lies.

## The Most "Lame" Excuses

Feeling that you are too old or too young or too sick or too busy may be a half-feasible excuse for not fasting. But some people have the most "lame" excuses imaginable for not fasting:

- Some actually think they are going to die if they fast. "Why take the chance?" they ask.

- Some feel like they are having some type of reaction, that they can't breath. "It's too hard for me," they say. And they discontinue their fast.

- Some intend to fast — next year. They always have good intentions, but for the future, not for today.

- Some actually fast — breakfast, lunch and dinner. Then they eat like pigs and fall into the bed to "sleep it off."

- Some people feel that it is enough to abstain from food from bedtime to break_fast.

- Some people cannot function without meat in their stomachs.

- Some people fast for wrong motives. If you want to serve God, serve Him with a pure motive. If you want to deny the flesh, then do it. Stop making excuses.

- Some people profess to fast just to please others. The truth is that on the way home they stop at Mc-Donald's and eat heartily. They think they are fooling someone. But you can't fool God. Fasting is not for the pleasure of other people. Fasting is done unto God.

  Sometimes we are led to call the entire church to fasting and prayer. If we were to look around at some of the local restaurants, I am afraid we would find a few people there cheating on God. In reality, they are cheating themselves. God doesn't benefit from your fasting. You are the one who benefits.

  This is a serious matter. Why play games with God? If you cannot be sincere in a fast, God won't be able to trust you with His blessings.

- Some don't fast because they will be "misunderstood" and they don't want to be criticized. Well, that's just part of it. It is wonderful to walk in the power and anointing of God. Some people may be critical of you. They may say that you are "anti-social." They may say many other unkind things. But when they have a need, they will know who to call on. When effective prayers must be prayed, they will remember your dedication to God. Don't let what other people think or say hinder you. Obey God.

Right now, TODAY, you must face the thing that has kept you from fasting and conquer it once and for all.

If gluttony has kept you from God's best, He is ready to deliver you from that sin. If FOOD is your Lord, cast it down from its throne today and let Christ reign and be the Lord of your life. If your BELLY has been your god, make Jehovah, God of our fathers, your God TODAY.

If you have a medical problem that prevents you from fasting, God is able to heal you. If His will is for His people to fast, and you are one of His children, His will is that you fast. And if you cannot fast because of a medical problem, He wants to remove that obstacle so that you can have total victory in your life. Be healed in the name of Jesus Christ TODAY.

If God is leading you to fast, then fast. Lay aside every excuse. Conquer the flesh, and **JUST DO IT**.

I congratulate those of you who have fasted in the past and those of you who have been challenged by this book and are about to embark on a journey into the realm of fasting and prayer and seeking the face of God. You will experience great breakthroughs in the Spirit. You are about to get control over your appetites once and for all. You are about to hear from God in a new and living way. You are about to have your faith increased.

First, let me give you some practical tips that will help you make the most of your fasting experience.

# Part V

# What to Expect from Prayer and Fasting (Action and Results)

# Chapter 17

## *Practical Things I Have Learned about PRAYER AND FASTING* (Action)

From my experiences with prayer and fasting, here are a few things that I would recommend to you that I believe will help you to achieve God's best for your life.

### During the first few days of your fast, don't ask God for anything.

Many people have the "gimmes." They only fast to get something material. They go to God with a wish list. Don't trivialize fasting. We do not fast only to receive an answer to a specific prayer. We fast for the sake of our spiritual position with God.

When you fast, seek to understand and experience the love of God. Other things will come. Begin by acknowledging His love and by expressing your love for Him. Worship Him. Adore Him. Glorify Him. Work toward a deeper expression of your mutual love.

---

We do not fast only to receive an answer to a specific prayer. We fast for the sake of our spiritual position with God.

---

What should you pray for during a fast? The same God who urges you to fast can burden your heart with the specific needs for which you should pray.

## Repent of your failings and shortcomings.

Acknowledge your failings and shortcomings. Confess them before the Heavenly Father and allow Him to cleanse your heart, to wash you clean. Most people have so many things that stand between them and God that they need several days just to clear the air and be ready to communicate well. Fasting is not just for the purpose of resolving specific problems. It has the purpose of renewing and strengthening your relationship with God so that your everyday prayers can be more effective.

Pray as David did:

> *Search me, O God, and know my heart; test me and*
> *know my anxious thoughts. See if there is any offen-*
> *sive way in me, and lead me in the way everlasting.*
> Psalms 139:23-24

If you fast, yet you have something in your heart against your neighbor — grudges, unforgiveness, bitterness, strife, envy, or backbiting — don't expect to get miracles from God. Any of those things will bring you into bondage — if they are allowed to rule in your heart. Use this time in prayer and fasting to bring these things to the light and to allow God to deal with them.

Some believers gossip too much and love to hear something bad about another brother. Some believers cause divisions in the Body of Christ. Some believers don't love their brothers and sisters. Let God search your heart and bring to light hindrances to answered prayer of which even you are not aware.

## Intercede for others.

Before you ask for things that you need yourself, pray the heart of God. Intercede for others. You won't lose anything by doing this. God is concerned about your most insignificant need, but He is concerned that you be like the One Who laid everything down to serve others. When you have prayed for others, the Father will stretch out His hand to you and invite you to receive all that you are personally lacking.

Intercede for the leaders of our society. Intercede for our community leaders. And intercede for our spiritual leaders. It is easy to criticize our leaders. The most lazy people can do that. But few are willing to give the time and effort necessary to intercede in prayer for those in authority. If we believe that God is powerful, we should be willing to ask His help in every matter, both public and private. If we believe that old saying: *PRAYER CHANGES THINGS* (not God), then let's put it to work.

We are admonished by Jesus Himself to pray for more laborers for the spiritual harvest. If we should pray for them to get into the harvest, surely we can uphold them during their labors in the field. They are human, and they will make mistakes. But we are not called to judge them. God is the judge. We are called to uphold God's servants in prayer.

Because we live in a democratic society, we, as beleivers, often take to extremes the liberty we have to criticize. Deacon boards and other elected bodies of representatives in our churches often take an adversarial role, very much like an opposition party in Congress or some European parliament. This is not God's way. We are all in the same party. We are all members of the same Kingdom. Support one another. Pray for one another. Intercede for one another.

## Boldly present your own needs before the Lord.

When you have taken these steps, it is time to present your needs before the Lord. You may do it with great boldness.

*Do not be anxious about anything, but in everything, by prayer and petition, with thanksgiving, present*

*your requests to God. And the peace of God, which
transcends all understanding, will guard your hearts
and your minds in Christ Jesus.*

Philippians 4:6-7

God shows His interest in your need by His concern
with your *"daily bread."* He wants to supply for you personally. Don't be hesitant to take your petitions before
Him. Do it boldly. God wants to help YOU.

*For he and all his companions were astonished at the
catch of fish they had taken,*      Luke 5:9

Peter was surprised when Jesus gave him the miraculous draught of fish. He hadn't learned yet that God is
interested in our smallest problem and wants to help us.

The story is a familiar one: Jesus saw two ships standing
by the shore. He got into one of them (which happened to
belong to Peter) and asked him to thrust the boat out a
little from the land so that He could address the entire
crowd at once. When He had finished ministering to the
crowd, He said to Peter, *"Launch out into the deep and let
down your nets for a draught"* (Verse 4 KJV).

Peter said, *"Lord, we have toiled the whole night and we did
not catch any fish but nevertheless at thy word, I will do what
You have commanded"* ( Verse 5 Paraphrased).

When he cast the net, it took in more fish then he could
handle, and his boat started sinking. The net was breaking
with the burden, and Peter had to call for help from another boat. What a lesson Peter learned that day!

God knows our needs. He is more than aware of our problems. He has declared that we need only ask Him, and He will rescue us in our hour of need.

Our problems serve the purpose of getting our attention. They make us draw near to God and cry out to Him. When we do, He is more than eager to hear our pleas and to help us.

Knowing this, learn to verbalize your need. This is something that many have not learned to do effectively. God's Word says: "*Ask*" (Matthew 7:7). He is anxiously awaiting your plea.

Don't get tired of praying, and don't be embarrassed to pray publicly. Elijah stood before his critics and boldly talked to his God. You can do the same.

## Concentrate on the Word of God.

Once you have begun your fast, **don't spend all your time in front of the television**. For one thing, too many foods are advertised on television. Without thinking, you might get up, go to the refrigerator, and get something to eat. The most important reason not to do it, however, is that television won't feed your soul.

Don't waste your time on magazines or other frivolous reading materials either. **Use this opportunity to get into the Word of God.** Meditate on God's promises. Let your mind dwell on them. Claim them for yourself.

The Word of God is true. We can trust its promises. It is never failing. If God's Word can fail, then He is no longer God. It is impossible. Believe Him.

*For the word of God is living and active. Sharper than any double-edged sword, it penetrates even to dividing soul and spirit, joints and marrow; it judges the thoughts and attitudes of the heart. Nothing in all creation is hidden from God's sight Everything is uncovered and laid bare before the eyes of him to whom we must give account. Therefore, since we have a great high priest who has gone through the heavens, Jesus the Son of God, let us hold firmly to the faith we profess.* Hebrews 4:12-14

The Word of God is so powerful that it can penetrate any obstacle, any circumstance, or any problem in life. It is more powerful than a two-edged sword. It can separate the spirit from the soul. It can slice into the thoughts and intents of the heart. Give yourself to the Word during your time of prayer and fasting.

## Don't neglect the prayer aspect of fasting.

The most important aspect of your fast is prayer; and there are several important things that you should consider in regard to prayer:

Our principle purpose in prayer is not to wrestle with the Enemy. If you allow him to, Satan will dominate your prayer time. The purpose of prayer is to communicate with the Father, to tell Him of our love, to worship and adore Him, and to intercede before Him for others. Don't let the Enemy dominate the conversation. Jesus taught His disciples to pray:

" 'Our Father in heaven ...' "            Matthew 6:9

He didn't teach us to spend all our time in prayer addressing demons and Satan. Satan has no right to interrupt our intimate time of fellowship with God. Cast him out. Send him on his way. Don't yield your valuable time to the Enemy.

> Submit yourselves, then, to God. Resist the devil, and
> he will flee from you.            James 4:7

> Do not give the devil a foothold.     Ephesians 4:27

Don't pray for the Devil to go. Command him to go. Use the authority God has given you. Put the Enemy in his place. Let him know that he has no right to disturb you while you are communing with the Father.

You may ask God for wisdom and authority to deal with the Enemy. Then, without wasting more precious moments, put him to flight and continue your private conversation with the heavenly Father.

Satan will oppose you as you pray.

> For our struggle is not against flesh and blood, but
> against the rulers, against the authorities, against the
> powers of this dark world and against the spiritual
> forces of evil in the heavenly realms.
>
>                         Ephesians 6:12

But, never try to debate with Satan. He can outsmart you every time. Don't listen to his arguments. He is a liar.

Don't entertain his thoughts. Don't let him finish his thought. Send him on his way. You have power, in the name of Jesus Christ, to cast him down.

Because Satan attacks them in prayer, some people spend a few seconds in actual prayer and the balance of their prayer time arguing with Satan. Rebuke him and let him know that he cannot waste your precious time.

Don't hesitate to bind any evil spirit that torments you during prayer and fasting. Don't ask God to take care of them. He has given you authority to take care of them. Don't be afraid. Speak directly to the demons. Bind them in Jesus' name. Command them to take their hands off of your family, off of your business, and off of your house.

Satan knows that he has no right to interrupt the activities of my home. He knows that the members of my family are covered by the blood of Jesus. He knows that he doesn't belong in our house. He knows to Whom we belong. He has no right to touch us, and I am not afraid of him.

## Get your mind on God.

Since Satan's goal is to get your mind on him and his activities, the most important thing you can do is get your mind on God. Be aware of His presence with you. Be conscious of His working in your life. If you just sit and let your mind wander, while God is trying to speak to you, you will never know His best for your life. If you let your mind wander, God can never reveal to you those better things that He has prepared for you.

Prayer is a two-way conversation. We speak to God, and God speaks to us. When God is speaking you must not be thinking about the score of your favorite football game or the current special offer at the corner restaurant.

Some people can actually quote scriptures, say the Lord's prayer, or do something else religious and, at the same time, be thinking about the most mundane things of life.

> *Let us then approach the throne of grace with confidence, so that we may receive mercy and find grace to help us in our time of need.*          Hebrews 4:16

## Learn to sense the presence of God.

Many people do not get their prayers answered because they cannot sense His presence; and how can you converse with Him effectively — if you cannot even sense His presence? These people cannot visualize Him; how could they talk intimately with Him?

When most people think about Jesus, they picture Him on the cross in agony. They weep for Him. They plead for mercy for Him. They ask the Father to be compassionate to Jesus. Because of this, they can't get any further in their prayers. How can Jesus help us if He is in agony Himself?

We must know that Jesus hung on the cross for a very short space of time. He was in the grave for a very short space of time. He overcame death. He overcame the cross. He overcame the grave. He is alive. He is not on the cross. See Him triumphant. See Him reigning.

**See Jesus**. Look into His face. Talk to Him. Tell Him your troubles. Confide in Him. Lay bare your soul before Him.

Don't think of Jesus as looking like some painting you have seen and liked. He is like nothing that any human has been able to capture with a paint brush.

Look to the Jesus of the Bible, not the Jesus of popular myth. He is the King of Glory. He is Lord of all. At His appearance, angels bow and say, *"Hosanna to the Lamb of God."* See the living God, and receive from His hand.

## Hold steady during the first few days.

Be firm during the first three days of your fast. They are the most difficult. It is during those days that many people quit. If you have a genuine burden for the lost, if you want to see drug addicts delivered and to see our society changed by God's power, you will continue. Be firm. When those first days have passed, it becomes easier to fast.

## Be aware of special needs.

**Some people need to get away from everyone while they are fasting.** The normal activities of the household might disturb their concentration. You don't need to go far or to spend a lot. Most churches have rooms that are not in use and that could be made available for a place of prayer.

Sometimes we need to get apart into a private place. My wife encourages me when I feel this need. She understands.

**Some people need to take time off from work to seek the face of God.** If we can take time off for vacations, for hunting season, or just to work around the house for a few days, why not do it for the welfare of our souls?

If you are married, **consider sleeping apart from your spouse while you are fasting.** Deny the flesh.

> *Defraud ye not one the other, except it be with consent for a time, that ye may give yourselves to fasting and prayer; and come together again, that Satan tempt you not for your incontinency.*
>
> 1 Corinthians 7:5 KJV

Agree with your spouse for a period of abstinence from your physical relationship for the purpose of seeking God. This will not hurt your relationship. It will strengthen it.

## Drink plenty of water while you fast.

Your body can go a long time without food, but it can only go a few days without adequate liquids. Since you will not be getting the liquids normally contained in most foods, drink a lot of water while you fast. Start drinking more, even before you start. It helps you to flush the poisons out of your system.

A fast is a good time to get free from your craving for sugar. Too many of us are addicted to sweets. And drinking plenty of water will help you get over this craving. Putting a little lemon or lime in the water may help.

When you go to the bathroom and urinate and your urine appears very yellow, don't worry. That shows that your body is flushing out the poisons from your system.

## Use wisdom when your fast has ended.

When your fast has ended and you begin to eat normally again, use wisdom. Some people do really crazy things. During their fast, they save back all the food they would have eaten and eat it later. After they finish the fast, they gorge and destroy all the good benefits they would have derived from the fast.

Begin to eat slowly, not all at once. And use the opportunity to develop better, healthier eating habits. Now that you have the flesh under control, this will be easier to do.

# Chapter 18

## *The Fruits Produced*
## *by*
## *Prayer and Fasting*
## *(Results)*

In the course of our search for truth concerning prayer and fasting, we have already discovered many of the benefits or results of this godly practice.

Prayer and fasting enable us to conquer the flesh and the selfish desires of our age and to walk in the Spirit of God. Prayer and fasting makes us sensitive to hear the voice of God so that we can gain the direction we need for our lives. Prayer and fasting opens our spirits to the supernatural and gives us the power and the anointing to work the works of God. Prayer and fasting sharpens our expectancy so that when we ask God for something, we expect to receive an answer. Prayer and fasting prepares us for the challenges of life, whatever they might be. Prayer and fasting enables us to adopt a more healthy life style and brings to us physical and mental health and healing (see also Psalm 35:13).

Many times confusion, anxiety and perplexity disappear after a person has fasted genuinely and sought the face of God. Prayer and fasting renews our minds. For those who want to attain growth through the knowledge of God's Word, fasting can help. Confidence to hold onto truth also comes about through prayer and fasting.

The patriarchs first discovered fasting. They fasted when they had bad news, such as times of mourning, sorrow, and affliction. For example, the case of Abraham for his wife Sarah (Genesis 23:2) and that of Jacob for his son Joseph (Genesis 37:34). Joshua and the elders of Israel remained prostrate before the Ark from morning until evening without eating after the Israelites were defeated by the men of Ai (Joshua 7:6). The Israelites, perceiving themselves to be pressed by the Philistines, assembled before the Lord at Mizpah and fasted in His presence until the evening (1 Samuel 7:6). In each case, God's people were comforted and received divine direction. Isaiah confirms that fasting will relieve you of heavy burdens (Isaiah 58:6).

In the early church, the believers fasted for much more than mourning, sorrow and affliction. For example, they fasted to be able to make quality decisions (Acts 14:23). The apostles ordained elders and prayed with fasting for them. The prophet Daniel also prayed and fasted for wisdom and received in (Daniel 10). Any person who does not consult with God in matters of serious decision making may be subject to poor judgement.

There are so many other blessings that prayer and fasting brings. Among them are:

Prayer and fasting brings revival and transformation. Historically, churches have been revived and transformed; cities have been revived; and entire societies have been revived — through serious prayer and fasting. The state of our nations cannot be changed solely through the political process. True change requires committed and dedicated warriors who know how to deal with spiritual powers unseen and unrecognized by our natural eyes. This knowledge comes only through prayer and fasting.

The whole world rejoices at the fall of communism and its evil influence. Contrary to popular opinion, this giant did not fall because of European political pressure, but as a result of the profound commitment of a few dedicated believers who gave themselves to prayer and fasting and the study of God's principles of successfully resisting the Enemy.

Fasting brings protection. When you are faithful to seek God in prayer and fasting and to commit your ways to Him, He will protect you from every enemy.

Fasting can usher you with success into a new project or a new ministry (Acts 13). When we enter into any new endeavor in this way, we are assured of the hand of God upon all that we do. Jesus began His ministry through prayer and fasting (Matthew 4:2). How much more we need to do the same! Businessmen should use this method of launching new business endeavors and of resolving difficult situations in their present businesses. Complex situations are often solved after prayer and fasting. Young people should use prayer and fasting to launch their careers. Students should pray and fast before selecting their courses of study.

Prayer and fasting helps us to understand the ways of God. Because He doesn't do things the same way every time, sometimes we have difficulty understanding Him. Tomorrow in God may be totally different than today. Prayer and fasting changes the way we perceive things. We begin to think more like God thinks, and so we can adapt better to His perfect ways.

Perhaps most important of all, prayer and fasting draws us closer to God. He is Spirit. Denying the flesh its desires for a period of time seems to shift the balance of power in our lives to the spiritual side. And the result is that we are close to God and more like Him. Those who pray and fast have a new hatred of unrighteousness and a new desire for God, His Word and the things of the Spirit.

## *My Prayer For You*

Friend, let me ask you: When was the last time you sought the face of God in prayer and fasting? If you are honest, you will recognize that you need God's grace. Let us believe God together as we pray.

*Heavenly Father,*

*I pray that the anointing of the Holy Spirit will rest heavily upon the words of this book. These are Your words. May every word come to rest in the hearts of Your people. And may every believer be stirred to action.*

*Help each believer to make a commitment to receive what You have spoken and to apply it to their every-day life.*

*Strengthen Your people! Encourage Your people! Cause Your people to rise up as a mighty prepared army that will go forth in Your power.*

*Give us power to overcome the appetites which endeavor to take control over our spirit life. Give us purpose and direction to follow You from this day forward.*

*In Jesus' Name I pray; and I thank You for the answer.*

*Amen!*

For another best-selling book
by Dr. Kingsley Fletcher, read:
***If I Were Satan.***

Books and tapes by Dr. Fletcher
may be ordered from:

**KINGSLEY FLETCHER MINISTRIES**
Miracle Life
P.O. Box 52209, Durham, NC 27717-2209
Phone: (919) 493-7662  Fax: (919) 471-0905